Love
mama

PRAISE FOR
PRAYER TAKES WINGS

Thetus Tenney has birthed a classic that offers a wealth of biblical insight and compelling stories about angels. Every believer should read this illuminating book.

BETH ALVES
President, Intercessors International
Bulverde, Texas

Thetus Tenney is a dynamic woman and a dynamic leader—because she is a dynamic woman of prayer. Read and be blessed by this testimony of the power of prayer, the link between you and God's unlimited resources.

JANE HANSEN
President and CEO, Aglow International
Lynnwood, Washington

Everyone needs a bit of heaven in their heart. This book opens a door to the reality that angels are in our midst! I love it!

CINDY JACOBS
Cofounder, Generals of Intercession
Colorado Springs, Colorado

Thetus Tenney has loved and served God for more than 40 years. She is a student of God's Word and has a passion for prayer. Prepare to be blessed by her insights about angels among us.

JOHN C. MAXWELL
Founder, The INJOY Group
Atlanta, Georgia

Like a jumbo jet lumbering down the runway, too heavy to lift off. That's how my prayers often feel. I can't get them off the ground, much less reach heaven! That's where this book helps. When you need extra "lift" in your prayers, here come the Lord's angels! As she's done since I was a little boy, my mom, Thetus Tenney, teaches me about the real wind beneath my wings.

Prayer Takes Wings will cause your faith to soar and your prayers to ascend. With stories of contemporary encounters and ample biblical precedence, the revelation quickly sinks in that angelic assistance is available to all God's children. Your prayer life will never be the same.

No longer will you desperately fling heavy prayers heavenward only to feel them dribble off your lips and crash to the floor. You will pray and "they" will fly! To paraphrase a popular song:

> I believe I can fly.
> I believe I can touch the sky.
> When I pray every night and day,
> They spread their wings and fly away.

Prayer truly does take wings! My mommy told me so.

TOMMY TENNEY
GodChaser and son of an earth angel
Pineville, Louisiana

Seasoned, mature saints can teach us certain things through their experiences that bring new and comprehensive dimensions to biblical truths like nothing else. This is the case as Thetus Tenney expounds with incredible insight and great biblical revelation on the ministry of angels to the Body of Christ. Your faith will rise to a new level as you read these outstanding testimonies of God's miraculous interventions through angels into people's lives. You will know beyond a doubt that even now God is using angels to answer your prayers.

DUTCH SHEETS
Author of *Intercessory Prayer* and *The River of God*
Colorado Springs, Colorado

PRAYER TAKES WINGS

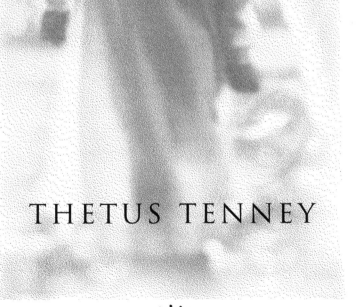

THETUS TENNEY

Renew

A Division of Gospel Light
Ventura, California, U.S.A.

Published by Renew Books
A Division of Gospel Light
Ventura, California, U.S.A.
Printed in U.S.A.

Renew Books is a ministry of Gospel Light, an evangelical Christian publisher dedicated to serving the local church. We believe God's vision for Gospel Light is to provide church leaders with biblical, user-friendly materials that will help them evangelize, disciple and minister to children, youth and families.

It is our prayer that this Renew book will help you discover biblical truth for your own life and help you meet the needs of others. May God richly bless you.

For a free catalog of resources from Renew Books and Gospel Light please call your Christian supplier or contact us at 1-800-4-GOSPEL.

Cover Design by Kevin Keller
Interior Design by Rob Williams
Edited by Kathi Mills and David Webb

Library of Congress Cataloging-in-Publication Data
Tenney, Thetus 1934–
        Prayer takes wings / Thetus Tenney.
            p. cm.
        ISBN 0-8307-2465-6 (pbk.)
        1. Angels.   2. Lord's Prayer—Criticism, interpretation, etc.   I. Title.
    BT966.2.T46 2000
    235'.3—dc21   99-056929

1 2 3 4 5 6 7 8 9 10 11 12 13 14 15 16 17 18 19 20 / 05 04 03 02 01 00

Rights for publishing this book in other languages are contracted by Gospel Literature International (GLINT). GLINT also provides technical help for the adaptation, translation and publishing of Bible study resources and books in scores of languages worldwide. For further information, write to GLINT, P.O. Box 4060, Ontario, CA 91761-1003, U.S.A. You may also send E-mail to Glintint@aol.com, or visit their website at www.glint.org.

DEDICATION

I dedicate this book to the memory of my oldest sister, Agnes Ruth Caughron Rich. Called to the ministry as a teenager, she continued for many years faithfully serving God, enjoying a special "ministry of angels" in her last 10 years of life. Perhaps there is a reason for that.

After establishing three new congregations and overseeing the construction of a building for each, she spent her final years building her fourth church in Grand Island, Nebraska. While there, my sister endured the destructive effects of a flood, a devastating tornado, a daughter's serious health problems and the deaths of her husband and our mother. She also broke her leg and ankle, suffered a severe financial loss and experienced a major heart attack, emergency open-heart surgery, two surgeries for cancer and a light stroke—all while she persevered through a four-year court case involving the Christian school sponsored by her church.

Throughout these trials, angels ministered to her repeatedly.

When I was a little girl full of fresh-eyed wonder, I learned a lot about prayer by following and kneeling with my sister in a tiny little church up on a hill. As a youth, I learned about women and the Word of God from watching my sister preach and serve. As a woman seeing through wiser eyes and nursing my own wounds of experience, Agnes taught me a lot about God and angels as I stood alongside her on the battlefield of life.

Prayer, the Word, God and His angels were always sufficient for my sister.

Me, too.

CONTENTS

FOREWORD

The Lord has spoken again to His handmaiden Thetus Tenney, this time about angels. And why not? We read about them in the Bible from Genesis to Revelation. They ministered much to the first apostolic Church in Jerusalem. Angels don't die; they are eternal beings, and so they minister to us even today.

How do we get angels to minister to us? When we preach the Word and pray the Word with the anointing of the Holy Spirit, angels immediately move in to minister:

Bless the Lord, you His angels,
Who excel in strength, who do His word,
Heeding the voice of His word (Ps. 103:20).

In 2 Corinthians 4:18, Paul tells us to look at things not seen. When we look at things seen around us today, all seems hopeless. In *Prayer Takes Wings*, the author stresses the biblical truth of the invisible realm, where God and His angels wait for the Church to wake up and pray until the heavens open and the power of God descends upon this world with a revival that will stagger the minds of men, shake the powers of hell loose from the nations and fill the whole earth with His glory.

Thank you, Thetus Tenney, for always being there when the Church needs you. May God's angels always encamp round about you until He comes.

T. W. B A R N E S

Thank you, T.W., for being my mentor and directing me on this journey into the spiritual realm of God and His angels.—T. T.

ACKNOWLEDGMENTS

I have my doubts whether one writes a book or "births" it. I do know it is a painfully joyous event. This book never would have been delivered without the capable and willing assistance of Nell Perry, Carolyn Fletcher, Pam Nolde, Karen Roberts, Fredi Trammell, Donnell Spurgeon and the special privileges granted me by my wonderful husband, Tom, who insisted I take the time to write *Prayer Takes Wings*.

This simplistic book on a supernatural subject has been in my heart a long time. Finally the time came to deliver it, and here it is for you, dear reader. My desire is that, first of all, this book glorifies the Lord to whom all power, honor and glory belong. And then for you, I hope this uncomplicated study on a seemingly incomprehensible subject convinces you that we have heavenly allies in the battles of everyday life, that it opens your mind to become more aware of the supernatural and that you must open your mouth to share the glorious workings of God and His angels among us.

Many stories about the ministry of angels have been shared with me over the years. I received them gratefully, and I have tried to retell them as nearly as possible to the original accounts.

ANGELS
WATCHING
OVER US

While serving as a member of the Louisiana Board of Elementary and Secondary Education, I attended a conference, sponsored by the Louisiana State Department of Education, which addressed the problems and needs of students. Workshops on alcoholism, drugs and abuse did not surprise me, but I wasn't expecting a session dealing with satanism among students.

Our culture has become increasingly interested in the spirit world. Demons, devils and witches are no longer relegated to Halloween but are now grabbing headlines and dominating conversations. Eerie stories, once reserved for late night "spook" parties, now command big bucks by the famous, who tell their stories and entice intelligent people into their otherworldly experiences. With no thought of ridicule, they tell of spirit guides, magic crystals and out-of-body experiences.

Belief in the supernatural soared in the late 1980s and throughout the '90s. In July 1989, an Associated Press (AP) article stated that 94 percent of America's teenagers believed in angels. Another AP article in September 1992 reported the following:

> Times have gotten so bad that guardian angels are turning up in individuals' lives with increasing frequency, and people are more receptive to the heavenly beings than ever before, say leaders of angel-related organizations and businesses. In the past year, guardian angel pins have moved from bins in the back of the Catholic bookstores to the check-out counter at card shops, florists and drugstores.

The article continued by reporting the establishment and growth of mail-order companies specializing in angel-related merchandise, and that several self-help books had hit the market to assist people in contacting their own personal angel. In Denver, when a specialty store called Angels for All Seasons opened, it did $150,000 in business the first four months.

Both *Time* and *Newsweek* magazines ran feature articles about angels in December 1993. According to *Time*, 55 percent of adult Americans then believed in angels or "higher spiritual beings created by God with special power to act as His agents on earth." The magazine quoted Peter Kreeft, a Catholic philosophy professor at Boston College, as saying, "These are desperate times. People seek supernatural solutions to their problems. We want to reassure ourselves of our spiritualism."

In December 1992, *Ladies Home Journal* asked readers to send in stories about their own angelic encounters. They received hundreds of letters and published several of them a few months later.

George Howe Colt, in his article "On the Trail of Angels" in the December 1995 issue of *Life* magazine, wrote that 69 percent of Americans believed in angels, "with 32 percent saying they've felt an angel's presence."

As we begin a new millennium, interest in angels is still on the rise. Angel websites have naturally surfaced on the Internet, at least three glossy national magazines devoted exclusively to angels are now being published, and "nonfiction" books about angels are flooding the market. Once reserved for the Christmas season, books on angels recently captured 5 of the top 10 slots on the paperback best-seller list.

There are numerous specialty stores and catalog houses devoted to angel paraphernalia, and universities such as Harvard Divinity School and Boston College are offering courses on angels, one of which is called "Angels, Angels: Some Fun Facts."

Following are excerpts from recent magazine articles on angels:

Believe it or not, over half the population (57%) say there are angels among us. Who believes in angels? 71 percent of all Americans, 76 percent of all teenagers, 78 percent of all women. Though women are more in touch with these heavenly spirits than men (65% vs. 48%), the winged guardians clearly have landed in America's consciousness (*Family Circle*, January 5, 1999).

David Sandler, 59, a clinical psychologist, has his own miraculous tale. Diagnosed with lymphoma and given three years to live, he lay in the hospital, close to death. But then Sandler heard a loud voice singing a Hebrew song he'd known as a child: "Hear O Israel, the Lord my God, the Lord is One." At that moment, he recalls, "I moved out of my body up to the ceiling. I felt that love I had for God when I was a child. I was as happy as I could be." Then, says Sandler, "I started sinking back, and it was a shock—the body I left is not the one I came back to." Later tests proved him right—Sandler was cancer free ("Heaven Help Us," *People*, 1999).

[When the] "Touched by an Angel" television series made its debut some five years ago, one critic called it "the season's worst new series" and the show almost canceled (*Good Housekeeping*, April 1997).

Today ["Touched by an Angel"], now into its fifth season, ranks most weeks as the second most-watched drama series in the Nielsen ratings (*People*, Top Stories/Heaven Help Us!/PeopleOnline/Touched by an Angel, February 22, 1999).

With the growing influence of this "spiritual" climate, it is important that Bible-believing Christians understand, expect and openly discuss the supernatural workings and prominent angelic activity of the kingdom of God, which can only be correctly comprehended through study of God's Word. The primary meaning of the Hebrew word for angel as used in the Bible (*mal'ak*) is "messenger"—in this case, a messenger sent by God to fulfill His purposes. Comforting words from Scripture and the blessings of worship can be enhanced by probing into the supernatural world of God and His angels. The true believer in Christ not only has the power to cast out demons, but can also expect to receive angelic assistance, whether seen or unseen, as described in Hebrews 1:14:

> Are they [angels] not all ministering spirits sent forth to minister for [serve, help] those who will inherit salvation [believers]?

THE UNSEEN WORLD

Time is an interlude in eternity that encapsulates mankind and our temporary world of the material. Our earthly existence is confined to an opaque bubble, which the apostle Peter tells us will someday dissolve and melt away:

> But the day of the Lord will come as a thief in the night, in which the heavens will pass away with a great noise, and the elements will melt with fervent heat; both the earth and the works that are in it will be burned up. Therefore, since all these things will be dissolved, what manner of persons ought you to be in holy conduct and godliness (2 Pet. 3:10,11).

Beyond our temporal world lies the eternal world of spirits and angels and God. Every man is connected to that otherworld by the tether of God's breath, which made him a living soul, a part of the invisible world.

Every Christian has the right to know that in the invisible world of spiritual powers, they who are with us are still more populous than they who are with the devil. This becomes evident when physical eyes are opened to the spirit world:

And when the servant of the man of God arose early and went out, there was an army, surrounding the city with horses and chariots. And his servant said to [Elisha], "Alas, my master! What shall we do?"

So he answered, "Do not fear, for those who are with us are more than those who are with them."

And Elisha prayed, and said, "Lord, I pray, open his eyes that he may see." Then the Lord opened the eyes of the young man, and he saw. And behold, the mountain was full of horses and chariots of fire all around Elisha (2 Kings 6:15-17).

When Satan was cast out of heaven and became the god of this world, he took with him a third of the angels, who would become his emissaries and cohorts of evil. This means that two-thirds of the angels remained in heaven to become ministering spirits to the heirs of salvation. According to my calculations, demons or fallen angels are outnumbered in the spiritual realm two to one! Timidity, reluctance and fear should melt away as we consider this innumerable company of angels who are on our side:

Then I looked, and I heard the voice of many angels around the throne . . . and the number of them was ten thousand times ten thousand, and thousands of thousands (Rev. 5:11).

It is awesome to consider that the Lord God, whom we serve and who uses the clouds as His chariots and walks upon the wings of the wind, can also make "His angels spirits, His ministers a flame of fire" (Ps. 104:3,4).

I love these words written by Ruth Graham in *Clouds Are the Dust of His Feet* (Wheaton, IL: Crossway Books, 1992): "Clouds are the dust of His feet and watching the evening sky I chuckled to think, *How neat. God just passed by.*"

The psalmist penned:

Bless the Lord, you His angels,
Who excel in strength,
Who do His word,
Heeding the voice of His word.
Bless the Lord, all you His hosts,
You ministers of His,
Who do His pleasure (Ps. 103:20,21).

PRAYER AND ANGELS

Prayer is our line of communication into the unseen world beyond the bubble of our earthly existence. It is the believers' daily privilege, because of the price paid with the shed blood of Jesus Christ, to go boldly into the throne room of God and, through our prayers, to seek help and to make our petitions and requests known (see Heb. 4:16). In His throne room are many angels—ten thousand times ten thousands and thousands of thousands, as recorded in the book of Revelation.

John's writing in Revelation exposes for us the dual world of corresponding activity between man's world and the spirit world. The prayers of the saints, precious and powerful, are shown to be held in the hands of angels (see Rev. 5:8; 8:3-5).

All heaven recognizes the authority of using the name of Jesus in prayer. When we pray in Jesus' name, according to God's will revealed by His Word, we can be sure of corresponding activity in heaven. The angels, in all of their glory, who excel in strength and might, must step aside and snap to attention when the voice of one saint whispers the prayer of the privileged, "Our Father. . . ."

While this book is by no means a comprehensive study of angels, it is intended to show the reality of angelic intervention in our lives and to clear the air for open discussion of the supernatural.

PART ONE

ANGELS

Chapter One

MORE
THAN MEETS
THE EYE

There is more here than meets the eye. This old adage could never be truer than when it is used in reference to the spirit world. Long ago at the city of Dothan, Elisha's young servant was terrified at the intimidating sight of the massive Syrian army surrounding the city. The old prophet prayed a simple prayer: "Open his eyes that he may see" (2 Kings 6:17). In response to Elisha's prayer, God allowed the servant to see into the spiritual world. There, fiery horses and chariots of the Lord's host filled the mountains. From this biblical passage we so often quote the awesome promise: "Those who are with us are more than those who are with them" (v. 16). Thank God for those who can see both angels and Syrians!

We do not have to be as old as a prophet (or even old enough to be employed by one) to see the unseen. In Little Rock, Arkansas, young Josh had accompanied his grandmother, Margaret Harden, to church for her regular prayer time. As she prayed, Josh prayed and played around his kneeling grandmother. Suddenly, he started desperately trying to get her attention. Hitting her on the shoulders he shouted, "Look! Look!"

"What is it, Josh?" his grandmother asked, rather annoyed.

"A big boy! A big, big boy!" he cried.

Margaret looked up and saw him standing at the corner of the platform—big indeed—a mighty angel!

For the believer there is proof enough that in the events of this world there is definitely more than meets the natural eye. When tribal war broke out in an African nation, a missionary family was caught in the crossfire. Each of the warring factions was anxious to gain control of the mission's property. One night one of the tribes surrounded the house and was closing in on the frightened family when, suddenly, they stopped and ran away. Puzzled, the family nevertheless gave thanks to God. They later learned from the natives that the invisible angels who were encamped around the godly people had suddenly become visible to their attackers. Large, bright and intimidating, the angels were a fierce sight to the tribal warriors, who never returned to harass the family. Similar reports have been received, not only from Africa, but from endangered missionaries in many hostile territories around the globe.

We need look no further than the Bible for many insights into angelic activity. They are busily involved in the affairs of heaven and earth. Jesus Himself referred to "the angels of God ascending and descending" (John 1:51). Just as with Elisha at Dothan, the Bible frequently allows us a glimpse at parallel activities in the spirit world and the natural world. Since angels have access to both, a close look at some of their activities as recorded in the Scriptures gives us wonderful assurance that we are not alone. For the servant of God, in every situation there truly is more than meets the eye.

ANGELIC APPEARANCES IN THE BIBLE

Jacob saw angels going and coming between heaven and earth on a ladder (see Gen. 28:12). In that same place, God visited him with promise and blessing. Jacob was far from home, but a ladder is used for quick, temporary access; it can be moved and dropped down anywhere. We are never out of range of God and His angels.

Jacob again found this to be true when, in obedience, he started back home to confront his brother Esau. It was a stressful trip. Fear clouded his mind with questions, so he prayed for deliverance and the fulfillment of God's promise. As he traveled with his band of servants, the angels of God visibly met him. When Jacob saw them, he declared, "This is God's camp." He then called the name of that place Mahanaim, meaning two hosts or two bands (see Gen. 32:1,2). The visible band of Jacob and his servants was joined by the angelic host as Jacob moved along the path of obedience.

On the other hand, the prophet Balaam stubbornly rushed headlong and headstrong, going against God's own word to him. On his way to market his prophetic gift for money, he became frustrated by the obstinacy of his donkey. Three times the donkey turned away from Balaam's intended path because, ironically, she saw what the prophet did not see: the Angel of the Lord, standing in the way with His sword poised for destruction (see Num. 22:20-33).

Abraham, in absolute trusting obedience, stood seemingly alone at the altar he had built, his knife in his hand and ready to thrust it into his only son, Isaac, his earthly link to the fulfillment of God's promise. But Abraham was not alone. The Angel of the Lord was watching and spoke to Abraham at that crucial moment, and Isaac was spared (see Gen. 22:10-12).

Who could know the thoughts and loneliness of Joshua as he approached the massive walled city of Jericho? Here he was, newly ordained to succeed the great Moses as leader of the multitudinous wandering tribes of Israel and given the task of leading God's people in battle against this impregnable city. Yet Joshua's obedience to all that God had commanded him brought a word from the Lord. While lost in his thoughts, Joshua's eyes made the crossover from the visible to the invisible, and he saw someone else—an unidentified warrior seemingly sizing up the situation:

> And Joshua went to Him and said to Him, "Are You for us or for our adversaries?"
> So He said, "No, but as Commander of the army of the LORD I have now come" (Josh. 5:13,14).

The Angel of the Lord then proceeded to give Joshua his literal marching orders and the promise of a highly unlikely victory for the Israelites. Obviously, there was a lot more going on near Jericho than Joshua could see with his natural eyes.

Isaiah's world changed drastically with the death of his friend, King Uzziah. We cannot be sure whether or not Isaiah was in the literal Temple or the temple of his own soul when the invisible suddenly became visible and he saw the throne—the real throne—occupied by the Lord. Instead of the grief of Isaiah's natural world he saw the flutter of the seraphim (angels) filling the place with worship (see Isa. 6:1,2).

Peter and Paul were both in isolating circumstances—one deep in prison, one lost on a raging sea—when they were visited by an angel of the Lord (see Acts 12:3-8; 27:21-24). Prayers had been said by the church on behalf of Peter, whereas Paul prefaced the revealing of the angel's message with an indication of his constant relationship with God. My question is this: Did the angel find these men in their dire circumstances or was the angel already there keeping charge over them?

King Nebuchadnezzar watched as Shadrach, Meshach and Abed-Nego were thrown into the fiery furnace. Then, in astonishment the king rose up to count four men in the furnace (see Dan. 3:19-30). The angel—one "like the Son of God" (Dan. 3:25)—accompanying the three young men had become visible. Years later, under similar circumstances, an angel protected Daniel in the den of lions (see Dan. 6:20-22). Praying in Babylon brought angelic involvement, which overruled the laws of the land that no mere human could change.

All of these incidents had in common one thing: There was more involved than what men could see with their physical eyes. Angels were there, ready to fight, to comfort, to deter, to rescue, to aide, to reassure, to deliver, to keep and to preserve. Think about it! Those involved could not know it, but angelic assistance was at the ready, just waiting to be revealed.

THE MINISTRY OF ANGELS

The ministry of angels continues to this day. As had been Alma Nolan's habit for so many years, on this night in the city of Minden, Louisiana, she knelt at the little vanity bench in her bedroom to pray before retiring. A widow living alone for several years, she always closed her prayer with this request: "Lord, send your angels to watch over me through the night. In Jesus' name, amen."

Turning to get up from her knees, she was startled to see a big man standing in her bedroom doorway, leaning against the doorjamb. Her mind raced to check the doors and windows, which she knew were all securely locked. Fearfully she stammered, "Wh-wh-who are you?"

With a warm, confident gaze he replied, "You asked for me to come, didn't you?"

In a moment of distraction, she looked again and he was gone. The daily invisible had become visible to a precious saint of God for a few moments. Prayer request granted!

We live in a material world of things we can see, touch and sense in our physical being. But just beyond a tissue-thin veil is the spiritual world where angels are very real and very busy. Occasionally the physical eyes are truly opened to see the reality of an angel. Oh, what an awesome sight would confront us if we could see as Elijah's servant saw! I am convinced we would behold an almost unbelievable number of angels, going and coming between the two worlds. And in our immediate surroundings we would see many angels watching, listening, observing, guarding, guiding, moving like the wind at the impulse of God's commands concerning us and our prayers.

Late in life the apostle John had been condemned to exile on the lonely, rocky, barren island of Patmos. But there was certainly more to his lonely existence than met the eye. John was "in the Spirit" (Rev. 1:10) when his loneliness exploded with the activity of angels and he envisioned the book of Revelation. John became clearly aware that not only can the invisible angelic beings of another world become visible in the natural world to instruct, guide or protect, they can also appear to us in dreams and visions to convey messages from God, to reveal God's plans or purposes.

Then one of the seven angels . . . came to me and talked with me, saying, "Come. . . ." And he carried me away in the Spirit to a great and high mountain, and showed me the great city, the holy Jerusalem, descending out of heaven from God (Rev. 21:9,10).

Angels can become visible at times, but they also speak to us through our dreams and visions. When they do, we somehow can enter into the reality of those visions and dreams. Isaiah, Daniel, Zechariah and Joseph all had angels appear to them in visions and take them into the reality of the invisible.

Helen Cole, who radiates God's love, has traveled the world preaching and singing. While Helen was visiting the Forbush family in Australia, Brother Robert Forbush had a very disturbing dream. In his dream, Helen fell. But just before she fell completely to the floor, four large men caught her. The next day Helen experienced a very dangerous fall, but miraculously she was not injured.

Several years ago we visited a wonderful group of believers in the mountains of Taiwan. A great revival had come upon these people, bringing such immense changes to the area that the police station was closed for lack of activity. When a bag of money was subsequently stolen from the church, the people were dismayed. That night in a dream, one of the men of the church saw someone hiding a bag of money under a little bridge. Early the next morning he gathered the elders and told them his dream. Hurrying to the bridge, they found the money exactly as the man had seen it in his dream.

To borrow a phrase from the apostle Paul, "We see in a mirror, dimly" (1 Cor. 13:12). I do not try to fully explain the supernatural, but I do know that in the events of our daily lives, there is more here than meets the eye.

CHAPTER TWO

ANGELS AT WORK

Angels are involved in the traffic flow of life—more specifically, in our lives. They are as near as God, who fills the universe and every crack and crevice of His world. They are part of the eternal, yet connected to time. What they have done as recorded in the Bible, they can still do today because they never die. They are immortal, and they never cease to serve God and minister to the heirs of salvation.

They can find and minister to a rejected woman like Hagar, who was lost in the wilderness of bitter despair (see Gen. 16:7,8); or a young woman of destiny like Mary, who lived in obscurity in a tiny village called Nazareth (see Luke 1:26,27); or women beset by the circumstances of life like Agnes Rich in Grand Island, Nebraska, or Alma Nolan in Minden, Louisiana.

Without the sophisticated technical assistance of radar, angels can locate Paul in a storm (see Acts 27:23,24), direct Joseph to protect his family (see Matt. 2:13) or suddenly awaken my husband, who was a thousand miles away from his family, to cover me and our children with prayer at the exact moment a tornado was moving toward our home.

Angels excel in strength (see Ps. 103:20) and can impart that strength to those in need (see Dan. 10:18). They can travel and transport effortlessly to move a preacher to his next assignment (see Acts 8:39) or a woman named Maude to the piano bench under a gospel tent. You will read about all these stories later in this book.

We have scriptural evidence that angels arrange appointments (see Gen. 24:7), give direction (see Acts 8:26), increase confidence (see Judg. 6:12) and warn people of danger (see Matt. 2:13), all in the daily course of life.

If angels have done all these things in the past—and more—they can still do them today. How much angelic activity do we miss because of the dust of time in our eyes? Our temporal vision is blurred, and we are therefore unable to know for certain if it was the same heavenly caterers with raven delivery service that fed Elijah by the brook and later gave him room service in the wilderness (see 1 Kings 17:6). Could it be that he was served by the same angelic company that soon after replenished the oil and flour every day for the widow (see 1 Kings 17:11-16)?

How did the money get in the fish's mouth to pay the Temple tax for Jesus and Peter (see Matt. 17:27)? How did the ax head swim (see 2 Kings 6:5,6)? Was the miraculous catch of fish a creative miracle or were aquatic angels involved (see Luke 5:4-7)?

Distinction between the activity of angels and the majestic, miraculous movements of God is often blurred. Such phrases as "the Angel of His Presence" (Isa. 63:9), "the Angel of the Lord"

(Judg. 6:11) and "the Angel of God" (Exod. 14:19) allow for discussion and speculation concerning theophanies (visible mani-
festations of God) and angels. I will leave such theological matters to others who are more scholarly than I. It is enough to
know that an awesome company of angels, the Lord's host,
moves at His command, and it matters not whether my prayer is
for bread or blessing.

Angels are involved in our lives. They observe us, and our
prayers activate them.

WHAT DO WE KNOW ABOUT ANGELS?

Until our knowledge is made complete in the age to come, we can
only know in part about many things. All we can truly know about
the supernatural and the work of angels represents only partial
knowledge. If we could know and explain it all, these things would
cease to be supernatural. However, we can glean some interesting
facts about angels from the evidence available to us.

Scripture tells us that angels are observant and curious and
that they experience joy and anger. Paul speaks of the angels
observing us (see 1 Cor. 4:9). Angels observed the beauty of creation and exulted with joy (see Job 38:7). Thousands of angels
witnessed the giving of the Law on Sinai (see Deut. 33:2, KJV).
Angels can be provoked, which is a serious infraction (see Exod.
23:20,21). When a sinner repents there is joy in the presence of
the angels (see Luke 15:7).

Angels are curious concerning the workings of salvation in
our lives (see 1 Pet. 1:12). Their observance of us is marked with
distinction. Jesus said that He will either honor or deny us before
the angels of God according to how we relate to Him in our
earthly lives (see Luke 12:8,9).

The angels will gather the elect (God's people) in the last days (see Matt. 24:31). A special "binding" power seems to be administered by the angels, as angels will be sent as reapers for the separation and binding of the tares and wheat (see Matt. 13:41,42). In Revelation 20:1-3, we read that it will take only one angel to bind the devil and cast him into the bottomless pit.

The Bible describes angels as mighty, strong, glorious, fearsome, wise, flaming. They move swiftly from place to place. They fight. They shout. They speak. They go before. They go behind. They can bless. They can destroy. They move through lightning, thunder, storms, earthquakes, hailstones and fire.

Angels of high order are assigned to watch over children (see Matt. 18:10). Others are assigned over the nations: "When God divided up the world among the nations, He gave each of them a supervising angel" (Deut. 32:8, *TLB*). They are fierce enough to make a king tremble and tender enough to comfort a lost boy.

Angels have tremendous power because they are propelled by God's Word, but their supernatural abilities are enlisted only at His command (see Ps. 103:20). Because Jesus refused to command them to come to His aid, an estimated 72,000 angels stood still while a few paltry soldiers and one betraying friend took Jesus captive (see Matt. 26:53).

It is almost mind-boggling to realize that these powerful beings are sent to minister to us, mere mortals yet the heirs of salvation (see Heb. 1:14). This should bring you wonderful comfort and assurance. To minister means to serve, care for, attend to, help, aid, assist, relieve, comfort, console, accommodate, befriend. What more could we need in this, the earthly track of our heavenly journey?

Angels are commissioned to provide us assistance, visibly or invisibly, consciously or unconsciously, in whatever way we need it. But beware! The angels of the Lord obey only His Word. *We cannot order or command His angels.* The heavenly hosts are activated by our prayers to God according to His Word or at His discretion.

Angelic intervention in our lives, whether known or unknown to us, increases as we become more Kingdom-minded and as our prayers are oriented to the promises in the Word. This seems reasonable because God is committed to His Word and His kingdom, both of which are sure and will endure for eternity, and the angels are His agents to help accomplish this.

Worship and praise, the primary function of angels, make us kindred spirits. When we are solely dedicated to seeking first the Kingdom, praying without ceasing and continually offering up the sacrifice of praise in worship, we are living in sync with the Holy Spirit of God and have all heaven and the angels behind us.

ENTERTAINING ANGELS

There is no clear way to explain why angels appear to certain people at certain times yet never become visible to most of us. We are cautioned in the Bible that we can entertain angels without being aware of it (see Heb. 13:2). Abraham and Lot did just that (see Gen. 18:1-22; 19:1-16).

It has been observed that angels may come to us in a dream, in a vision, in disguise as another person, in a thought or impulse. They come to us in a way to get their message across, not to draw attention to themselves. It is interesting to note that the women at the tomb saw angels (see Luke 24:4), but the disciples on the road to Emmaus recounted the women's story as a vision (see v. 23).

Our daughter Teri spent many years at home alone with her children, Shane and Shannon, while her husband, Steve, traveled in evangelistic ministry. Nights can be very lonesome, especially so in times of burdened distress.

In just such a time, tearful prayers followed her to bed one night. Drifting into sleep, she was jolted awake by the sound of footsteps on the small deck at the back of their mobile home. Fear came first, followed by a calming peace. The footsteps did not stop at the deck, but came on into the kitchen through the dining room, the living room and down the hall to her bedroom. With silent yet clear communication, she knew God had sent an angel to comfort and protect them. She fell into a peaceful sleep.

As long as Steve continued to travel, the angel returned occasionally, following the same path, outside on the deck, inside and down the hall. Her worries would subside and she would fall asleep in peace.

Years later, while recovering from a frightening, near-fatal viral attack, the angel returned in the same way, but in a different house, coming through the front door, the entrance, the dining room and to the door of her bedroom to bring peace and assurance during a traumatic time.

A friend of mine, who had been through divorce proceedings and the ensuing financial upheaval, was likewise visited in his time of devastation. From out of nowhere, it seemed, two strange men approached him. Their time was as brief as their message: "God loves you!" My friend's circumstances did not miraculously change, but he did. Simple utterance, super strength, supernaturally.

ANGELS AND OUR PRAYERS

Angels dwell in eternity with an infinite God. What we can know about them assures us that they are very interested in us, receive assignments pertaining to us and carry out God's commands concerning us.

We may feel very detached from the ethereal world in which the angels live, but we are so very easily connected. Prayer is our line of communication from the secular, materialistic world in which we live to that invisible realm in which God and His angels dwell. If you review all the incidents of angelic involvement mentioned in this book, whether biblical or more contemporary, you will discover that prayer is usually the catalyst for enlisting the assistance of angels.

All of our prayers are directed to God, *never* to angels. Not only is there the scriptural warning against worshiping angels (see Col. 2:18), but prayers to angels would be useless because they receive commands from God alone and move according to His word. An angel came with an answer to Daniel's prayer, but isn't it interesting and reassuring that Daniel's prayer was so important in the spiritual world that the angels fought for it for 21 days (see Dan. 10:12,13)?

I am convinced that there is no way to separate angelic activity from the workings of God. I certainly believe in an almighty God, and I also believe in angels. I also know that Abraham, Daniel, Cornelius and the Jerusalem church prayed to God and that He answered via an angel each time.

The Bible records no specific prayer by Gideon (see Judg. 6:11,12) or Paul on the ship (see Acts 27:23,24) or Mary at the annunciation (see Luke 1:26,27), but as anyone who truly prays knows, prayer is much more than uttered words. It would therefore be a mistake to conclude that these individuals were not praying. Sighs, groans and searching of the soul are heard by God as prayer (see Rom. 8:26), and angels can be sent in answer. Abraham's prayer dispatched an angel to Lot (see Gen. 18:22—19:29). Hezekiah's prayers resulted in a destroying angel being sent into the midst of the Assyrian army (see 2 Kings 19:15-19,35). Was not God behind these interventions?

The attack of the enemy had been fierce and discouragement had seized our son Tommy and his wife, Jeannie, in Lafayette, Louisiana, where Tommy pastored. Unbeknownst to them, my husband and I interceded in prayer for them and asked God to send to them a ministering angel. The next day Tommy called. There was a hush to his voice. "Mom," he quietly said, "something very special happened to Jeannie and me last night. God sent an angel to us."

Angels know the address for our prayers.

It would be surprising, I am sure, if all the events in the Bible were unfolded for us to see openly the corresponding activities of the spirit world. Could it be simply that whatever God does in the spirit world He does with the assistance of angels, just as whatever He does in our world He does with the assistance of men?

Two worlds—dramatically different, inexplicably intertwined—and God rules in both. The connecting link is prayer, an expression from our limitations to the unlimited resources in God.

SPECIAL ANGELS

From what we see in the Scriptures, it seems there is a hierarchical order to the angels' organization and that specific angels are given specific assignments.

MICHAEL

Michael is the archangel (see Jude 9). He alone carries this title. From the meaning of the prefix "arch," we can assume that he is the chief angel. Some scholars believe that before his fall, Lucifer was considered to be of equal rank, or even superior to, Michael and that Michael is the chief contender in warfare with the fallen one now known as the devil. It is interesting to note that Michael does not rebuke Satan but appeals to God (see Jude 8-10).

Michael is also apparently charged with special duties concerning the Jews, God's earthly people (see Dan. 12:1). The possibility exists, since some consider the Church to be "spiritual Israel" and/or because we have been grafted into the believing Jewish remnant, that Michael's special charge extends to all Christians today. It may have been Michael who cast Lucifer out of heaven. In Revelation 12 we see Michael leading the war against Satan (see vv. 7-10), and he will continue to war against our foe until Satan is finally consigned to eternal torment in the lake of fire (see Rev. 20:10).

During Desert Storm (the Persian Gulf War), Tom Barnes was sitting in his office talking to Morton Bustard when the telephone rang. Sylvia Clark, a prayer warrior from a distant state, was on the line. She explained that while she had been praying the Lord told her to call and tell him, "The Lord raised you up to pray for the Jews. Israel, the apple of my eye, is now in danger. Pray!"

Hanging up the phone, Brother Barnes thought perhaps he would ask Brother Bustard to pray with him, but something held him back. In a few minutes missionary E. L. Freeman walked into the office. Brother Barnes sensed immediately it was now time to pray. The three of them joined hands and began to pray for God to send Michael, the warring angel, into this war to confuse and defeat the enemy and to protect Jerusalem. They felt a mighty presence of God.

During the time they were praying, evangelist Mike Braswell was sleeping in his travel trailer that was parked behind the church. Later in the day he told Brother Barnes, "I had the strangest vision. I saw angels descending into Jerusalem." Brother Barnes felt this was confirmation that God had heard their prayers (along with the prayers of others) and had sent His angels to deliver His people from danger. Once again, God spared Jerusalem.

GABRIEL

Although considered by many to be an archangel along with Michael and perhaps Lucifer before his fall, the angel Gabriel is never identified in the Bible as an archangel. However, Gabriel appears to be the foremost of the messenger angels. He is obviously an angel of high rank, given the nature of his assignments and the fact that he is mentioned by name four times in the Scriptures.

Gabriel appeared twice to Daniel and brought him messages and understanding concerning the events of the end times (see Dan. 8:16; 9:21). He also appeared to Zacharias and to Mary, announcing the coming births of John the Baptist and Jesus (see Luke 1:13-31). His announcement of the birth of Christ, the incarnate Son of God, affords Gabriel a prominent place in the Bible and in our hearts.

SERAPHIM AND CHERUBIM

In addition to the archangel Michael and Gabriel and the messenger angels, seraphim and cherubim are two other types of angelic beings mentioned in the Scriptures. Seraphim and cherubim seem to be primarily assigned to worship and glorify God. They are surrounded in mystery and strangely beautiful by description. Isaiah gives us insight into the seraphim (see Isa. 6), while Ezekiel gives insight into the cherubim as living creatures (see Ezek. 1:5-24).

Seraphim appear to be special attendants to the throne of God, being positioned over it, and are engaged in continuous worship. When Isaiah in his vision entered the throne room of God, a seraph purified him with a coal from the altar. Man's approach to God's throne is always by the altar. Before the altar and surrounding the throne are a myriad of angels. In Revelation 5:11,12 and 8:1-5, we see thousands and thousands of angels before the throne and we see an angel offering incense with the prayers of the saints at the golden altar. We have scant knowledge of the involvement of these throne-room attendants with our prayers and our approach to the throne of God, but from the Scriptures we do know that they are involved. With what we can glean from Isaiah 6, it seems the seraphim are anxious to assist us in coming into communion with God.

The primary assignment of the cherubim is apparently to be the guardian attendants of God's throne and glory:

The Lord reigns;
Let the peoples tremble!
He dwells between the cherubim (Ps. 99:1).

Cherubim were also set to guard the way to the tree of life in Eden after man's fall (see Gen. 3:24). It seems they guard against unauthorized access to God. This is not solely a negative position. The mercy seat from which God communed with Israel was guarded on either side by the form of a cherub (see Exod. 25:18). Only when the blood of the sacrifice was present was there open access to God.

Similarly, by the blood of Jesus spilled at Calvary we can now have access to the presence of God. Praying in the name of Jesus not only enables us to pray with power, but that name in prayer also assures us access to God through our Savior's blood. When we come before God's throne with prayer in the name of Jesus, and by the blood of His atonement offer the sacrifice of praise and true worship, not only are we granted access but the seraphim and cherubim must welcome us.

MESSENGERS OF GOD

Perhaps the most common angelic assignment is that of messenger. From Genesis to Revelation there is a whir of angels' wings as they move back and forth, descending and ascending from heaven to earth and back, obeying the commands of the Lord. We often speak of angels' wings. Recorded in many places, the Bible refers to their wings and declares that angels do fly. Some of this is probably figurative to depict the amazing mobility that angels possess (see Ps. 18:10).

Angels serving as messengers may appear in various forms. They may appear as heavenly celestial creatures, as when they announced the birth of Jesus to the shepherds in the fields (see Luke 2:8-15), or they may appear in the form of a man, as when the Angel of the Lord appeared to Joshua. They may not appear at all but may only speak, as the Angel of the Lord called to Hagar out of heaven (see Gen. 21:17). In the midst of a traumatic event, David looked *up* and saw an angel (see 1 Chron. 21:16). An angel instructed Cornelius, by way of a vision, to send for Peter (see Acts 10:3-8). It is also possible for angels to deliver a message without appearing or speaking, as was the case of Balaam and his donkey (see Num. 22:23,24).

Hagar's angelic encounter illustrates the multifaceted ministry of these heavenly messengers. As I have already stated, I do not think we can ever clearly comprehend the ministry of these celestial beings, but the angel(s) came to Hagar as a messenger bearing a message, as a caring minister supplying water and as a warrior who afforded protection to her son (see Gen. 21:17-19).

I do not know if one or more angels were involved. I cannot separate what was directly done by God alone, apart from the angelic assistants. Nevertheless, I do know that God heard Hagar's cry and sent an angel on assignment who took care of her situation.

ANGELS AT THE END OF TIME

Just as the angels were present at creation, they will be present and involved in the culmination of all things. They are committed to God's kingdom and will assist in bringing all prophecy to pass in order to usher in the time when Jesus is crowned King of kings.

An angel will declare that time shall be no more (see Rev. 10:5,6). In the last chapter in the Bible, the angels are involved in the closing of this age (see Rev. 22:6,7,16-21).

In His discourse on the Mount of Olives, Jesus told His disciples that when He returns, He will do so with a heavenly entourage of holy angels (see Matt. 25:31). Paul observed in his second epistle to the Thessalonians, "The Lord Jesus is revealed from heaven with His mighty angels, in flaming fire" (2 Thess. 1:7,8).

Thus we may conclude that from the beginning and into eternity, the angels of God are very much a part of God's plans and purposes. Scripture shows these wise and wonderful creatures functioning as worshiping, warring, ministering and messenger angels, and reveals that among these classifications there is rank and authority.

Four times in the Scriptures, David is compared to an angel (see 1 Sam. 29:9; 2 Sam. 14:17,20; 19:27). When we consider that David was chosen by God to establish an everlasting dynasty, that he was a wise ruler and is considered by many to be the

Bible's foremost worshiper, that he was a warrior of distinction and a messenger of God's own heart, we can readily understand why the Lord would compare David to an angel.

CHAPTER THREE

ANGELS
ON
ASSIGNMENT

The Bible teaches that there are myriad celestial beings created by God (see Col. 1:16). They are innumerable (see Heb. 12:22)—ten thousand times ten thousands and thousands of thousands (see Rev. 5:11). I have heard it speculated that there could be up to a hundred trillion angels. They are of a different order of creation than we and are not restricted as are people by their physical limitations. Angels excel in strength, knowledge, wisdom and mobility. They are the created inhabitants of the heavenlies, and their principle business is to serve God and His purpose in the heavens and the earth. Ample examples of their activities are described to us in the Bible, where they are mentioned or alluded to more than 300 times.

Angels are ministering spirits sent to aid and assist the heirs of salvation (see Heb. 1:14). They are spirit beings who can assume a physical appearance. It is awesome that these heavenly beings who exceed our humanity are designated to be our aides. Unregenerate man is made lower than the angels, but in our redeemed state we are elevated above the heavenly hosts (see Ps. 8:4-6). As heirs to this position in God's kingdom, our needs are served by angels, according to the Word of God. This in no way allows us to take control of angels, for they are under the express control of God and do their work only at His command.

> The Lord has established His throne in heaven,
> And His kingdom rules over all.
> Bless the Lord, you His angels,
> Who excel in strength, who do His word.
> Heeding the voice of His word.
> Bless the Lord, all you His hosts,
> You ministers of His, who do His pleasure (Ps. 103:19-21).

Angels not only move and act at the spoken command of God (see 1 Chron. 21:27), but it seems they serve the purpose of God through general assignments. They are given orders to protect us physically, as we see in Psalm 91:11:

> For He shall give His angels charge over you,
> To keep you in all your ways.

Here is one of those stories about angelic intervention that many would find hard to believe without tangible proof. During the rebel fighting in the Philippines a few years ago, the rebels shattered one of the worship services of a church with a wild shooting spree. When the skirmish was over, a young girl stood in their midst, her dress riddled with bullet holes, yet she was physically unharmed by the attack. I have seen the dress and know this story to be true.

Angels are also ordered to protect us spiritually. As warriors, they encamp around us to deliver us from evil (see Ps. 34:7). A young man told the story of how he wrestled with a particular temptation. In his dream (possibly a vision) he saw himself completely surrounded by angels. Beyond them was the object of his temptation, but he was safe within the circle of angels. After a while, he made a move toward the temptation. When he did, the angels parted, opening the way. Terrified, he awoke to the realization that, although he was safely surrounded by angels, he could choose whether or not to stay within their protective circle.

Angels are defenders of God's people. On several occasions in the Bible, they join a conflict on earth from their heavenly position (see Judg. 5:20; Isa. 37:35,36).

While angels cannot preach the gospel, they are often sent to assist those who do. An angel assisted Cornelius in finding the preacher who could open the door of salvation (see Acts 10:1-6), and it was an angel who arranged the meeting of the Ethiopian eunuch with Philip, who in turn preached Jesus to him (see Acts 8:26-38).

As we have already seen, messenger angels abound in the Bible. Angels were dispatched with messages for Abraham, Hagar, Moses, Joshua, Elijah, Manoah, David, Isaiah, Daniel, Zechariah, Joseph, Mary, the three women at the tomb, Paul, John and others. And as we have also seen, their ministry to us has not ceased.

In the little community of Provencal, Louisiana, the Kinsey girls left their house and started across the street. Simultaneously, in Lafayette, a city about a two-hour drive south of Provencal, my daughter-in-law, Jeannie Tenney, was leading a women's prayer meeting. Suddenly, a message flashed through her mind to pray for the Brian Kinsey family. Moments later, with brakes screeching, a car hit one of the girls, but she was spared what could have been instant death. Did God speak to Jeannie to pray? Did one of His messengers race to enlist an intercessor? Was an angel on hand to prevent the death of that girl?

ANGELIC DELIVERY SERVICE

Angels get around, but their mobility is apparently not limited to themselves. David spoke of 20,000 chariots, implying the presence of thousands of warring angels (see Ps. 68:17). Elijah enjoyed this same type of angelic chariot service (see 2 Kings 2:11), and Elisha benefited from it as well (see 2 Kings 6:17). Philip had a one-way ticket with this transportation service (see Acts 8:39), and the beggar Lazarus was carried by the angels upon his departure from this world (see Luke 16:22).

One of the most wonderful stories I have ever heard concerns the young Maude LaFleur, who related this story after she was along in years. It happened in the early 1900s, when the first sweep of the Pentecostal experience was moving across the land. Maude was part of one of the "bands," as they were then called. A band consisted of several people who accompanied an evangelist to various communities or towns to help in a revival campaign. Maude was the pianist. The meeting place was quite a distance from where they were staying, and since they had no other means of transportation, it was necessary to leave earlier in the day to make the long walk in time for the night's service. But on this particular afternoon, Maude was having a "bad hair day," and the group (undoubtedly men) grew weary and impatient waiting for her. "You all go on and I'll hurry to catch up with you," the frustrated Maude told them. Everyone left the house while Maude, still seated with brush in hand, anxiously peered into the mirror.

After a long walk, the band approached the tent just in time for the service to start. They heard someone playing the piano but couldn't imagine who it might be, since Maude was the only pianist for the revival. When they entered the tent, they were shocked to see Maude playing the piano. She had never joined them on the road and certainly had not passed them.

"How did you get here?" they asked.

"I don't know," she replied. "One minute I was sitting on the vanity bench finishing my hair, then suddenly I realized I was sitting on the piano bench, so I just started playing!"

FEAR NOT

And there were in the same country shepherds abiding in the field, keeping watch over their flock by night. And, lo, the angel of the Lord came upon them, and the glory of the Lord shone round about them. . . . And the angel said unto them, Fear not: for, behold, I bring you good tidings of great joy, which shall be to all people (Luke 2:8-10, *KJV*).

Angels in the Bible have a tendency to denounce fear upon their arrival in the presence of humans.

"Joseph, son of David, do not be afraid" (Matt. 1:20).

"Fear not, Zacharias" (Luke 1:13, *KJV*).

"Do not be afraid, Mary" (Luke 1:30).

"Fear not, Paul" (Acts 27:24, *KJV*).

Angelic involvement does not always mean deliverance from a situation; angels may only be present to deliver us from the fear.

When angels ministered to Jesus in the garden on the night before His crucifixion, Jesus was not saved from death, but He was given strength to face the coming ordeal. When the angel stood by Paul on the storm-swept boat, the fear was denounced even while the storm raged on.

ANGELS OF DEATH

Angels not only bless, protect, guard and defend humanity; they are sometimes sent for the purpose of heralding or hurling destruction, death and doom. The firstborn of Egypt were wiped out and the entire country devastated with one pass of "the destroyer" (Exod. 12:23).

Psalm 78:49 describes this seemingly negative assignment of angels as "sending angels of destruction among them." Moffatt translates this same passage to read "the messengers of woe."

One angel destroyed 185,000 Assyrians in one night (see 2 Kings 19:35). In the book of Revelation, woes and judgment repeatedly come at the hands of angels (see, for example, Rev. 14:6-12; 16:1-21). When David sinned, God sent a pestilence, which came upon the land as an angel with a sword in his hand and killed 70,000 people (see 1 Chron. 21:14-16).

ANGELS OF COMFORT

My close friend Ima Kilgore and I share a love for the ministry of angels. One of the most awe-inspiring stories I have heard is one that involved Ima's precious mother-in-law. This old-time saint of God traveled for many years with her preacher husband, holding revivals and starting new churches.

In the early 1900s, education was at a premium. Mom Kilgore never attended a day of school. She could not read, not even a letter from her children, but she loved the Word of God. Every day, at various times, she would sense God's presence and pick up her Bible. Then she would sit in her chair and, with her Bible in her lap, look at the pages, softly turning them at a paced rhythm. Although she could not read, daily into her ears came a soft voice reading the words to her. She explained, "My angel reads it to me."

In the dedication of this book I mentioned the angelic visits to my oldest sister, Agnes. One particular angelic visitation is especially precious to me. Agnes had suffered serious health problems for 10 years. Every year seemed to bring more time spent in hospitals. Of the last 24 months of her life, 14 were spent in a hospital room.

About a year before she died, during one of her extended stays in the hospital, Agnes had grown weary and weakened but was still mobile. I had come to Monroe, Louisiana, for a few days to assist in caring for her and alleviating some of her loneliness. At night I stayed at my dad's house, enjoying some time with him and Mama Eunice and sharing our grief over the seemingly inevitable. Our routine was that when Agnes would awaken in the morning, she would call us. This prevented our waking her from her much-needed rest. One morning, I answered her phone call, and instantly I knew something had happened. She was not her usual chipper self and when I inquired as to what was wrong, she started crying.

"What's wrong, Agnes? What's happened?" I asked.

"He came again this morning."

"Who came? The doctor? What did he say?"

"No, not the doctor. My angel came again this morning."

My heart was beating wildly. "What did he say? Tell me about it."

"Well, for some unusual reason the night nurses finished all their shift duties early. They had even given me my morning bath before 6:30, told me good-bye, left the room and closed the door. I was just lying here in my bed, wide awake and quiet, when he came in the door."

"Did you actually see him this time? What did he look like? What did he do?"

"Oh, yes, I saw him very well. He was dressed in white and was so tall and big. His eyes were warm and deep, like nothing I've ever seen before. He walked over to the side of my bed and stood there gazing at me."

"Were you frightened?" I asked.

"No. He looked at me with such kindness and tenderness. Then he moved around the end of my bed to the other side, while all the time his eyes were on me. After a few minutes standing on that side, he walked back to the other side and sat down on the edge. He reached out and took my hand."

"Did he say anything?"

"No, he just sat there smiling at me and holding my hand."

Then I asked her the same question I always asked when she told me of an angelic visitation. "Why didn't you ask him something? Why didn't you talk to him?"

"You don't understand, Thetus. You just don't want to talk; you just don't have any questions when he is there."

"How long did he stay?"

"Oh, I don't know. Ten minutes, maybe. And would you believe it was after the shift change but no one, neither nurse nor aide, came into my room while he was there. But Thetus, that's not the best part. . . ." Her voice trailed off into tears. "The best part is what happened next. He finally stood up. He just stood there for a minute looking at me with those beautiful eyes. Then he slipped his big arms under my body, and when he did we both began to rise toward the ceiling. As I looked, his head almost touched the ceiling. Then he gently laid me back on my bed and said, 'I wanted you to know how it will be when I come for you.'"

"Agnes, were you literally lifted off the bed?"

"Oh, yes. I was suspended, resting in his arms. I was totally conscious of it."

From that day on I prayed that God would let me be with her when her angel came to take her home. I didn't articulate it, but I was hoping I could see the angel when he came.

By late summer of '93, Agnes was further weakened and miserable. All the family was staying as close as possible. I spent every day I possibly could at the hospital. Dad was 90 years old and limited in strength, so there were only the three of us— Jeanette (the only one of us who lived in Monroe), Billie and myself—to carry the load of responsibility in caring for Agnes.

I went home for a special service on Sunday evening, September 12, to assist in the opening of a seminar with John Maxwell on Monday morning. Monday evening I returned to Monroe with the intention of coming home Tuesday evening to be there for the final day of the seminar on Wednesday. Late Tuesday afternoon I packed my things into the car, told Dad and Mama Eunice good-bye and headed back to the hospital before leaving for the two-hour drive home. We had hired an attendant, a woman from the local church, to stay with Agnes through the nights; it was important for me to be home on Wednesday, but I began to feel very agitated about leaving. Agnes was feeling about the same as she had been, and I had plans to come back in a day or two; but I was torn, weighing one responsibility against another. Finally, with a very definite sense, I knew I must stay with Agnes. A great peace came over me.

I napped on a cot not more than two feet from her bed, her face turned toward me. Around four o'clock in the morning,

September 14, 1993, I sat up. As I did, her breathing stopped. The attendant, who was across the room, also sat up. I said, "She's gone." Every member of the family in the city woke up at the same time. Her angel had come and gently lifted her up, this time beyond the ceiling. Like Lazarus, she was carried away by an angel. No, I didn't see him, but I was keenly aware of his presence. An overwhelming peace held back my tears.

Agnes had shared her angel experiences with many of the hospital staff over the long months. In a place where death is a daily occurrence, Agnes's room filled up with nurses, aides and other staff members from the various floors where she had been a patient. Peace, stillness, love and silent tears witnessed the fact that we were standing where angels had stood. Almost an hour later a young man from the lab downstairs rushed into the room. "She was my all-time favorite patient," he said as he leaned over to kiss her cold cheek. "I always enjoyed coming in here."

Just a few weeks prior to her death, Agnes, by now so weak and sick from the complications of medication, briefly told me that her angel had come again for just a few minutes. Anxiously I waited for her to tell me about it, but all she said was, "You can't know. It was just for me." I wonder if he had made an appointment for a special assignment.

PART TWO

ANGELS AND OUR PRAYERS

THE LORD'S PRAYER

Our Father which art in heaven,
Hallowed be thy name.
Thy kingdom come.
Thy will be done in earth, as it is in heaven.
Give us this day our daily bread.
And forgive us our debts, as we forgive our debtors.
And lead us not into temptation, but deliver us
   from evil:
For thine is the kingdom, and the power,
And the glory, for ever. Amen.

Matthew 6:9-13 (*KJV*)

CHAPTER FOUR

OUR
FATHER

In the pattern prayer that Jesus taught His disciples, as recorded in Matthew 6:9-13 and Luke 11:2-4, every phrase, although simple, direct and very concise, surges with significance for sufficiency through prayer.

As I became more intrigued with the study of angelic involvement in our lives and prayers, I was blessed to discover that there are scriptural references concerning angelic involvement with every phrase of the Lord's prayer. Jesus' prayer is more than a beautiful piece of memory work for recitation. It is an agenda for prayer. What comfort and assurance to realize that as our prayers enter the throne room of heaven, there are millions of angels ready and available to become involved in God's will and His response to us.

"WHEN YOU PRAY, SAY . . ."

"Our Father." Thus begins the prayer of the privileged. What an awesome honor to take wings on the words of prayer and speak directly to Him who occupies the whole of the heavens, to become as one with the comfortable intimacy of a child with his father. It wasn't just happenstance that Jesus said to His disciples, "When you pray, say: Our Father in heaven" (Luke 11:2).

In the inner sanctum of the Upper Room shortly before His arrest, Jesus comforted His disciples with the intimacy of the Father-child relationship. Twenty-two times in chapter 14 of John, He used the word "Father" as He promised that they would not be forsaken in their fears nor left alone comfortless, as orphans.

With this relationship come some powerful privileges. Because we can call God our "Father," we are protected by a heavenly secret service agency: the hosts of angels. They are committed to watching over the children of God.

I fondly recall an incident when President John F. Kennedy was occupying the Oval Office. In this impressive office where powerful world leaders moved with rigid protocol, the president's children, Caroline and John, Jr., were photographed at complete ease. Caroline, shuffling along in her mother's high heels, had come in to see her father. Young John-John was peeping out from his imaginary world under the president's desk. The photographs warmed the hearts of millions because they depicted the comfortable relationship between a father and his children. The power of this particular father enhanced the privileges of his children, affording them special access and protection.

When we enter the throne room of heaven on the wings of prayer and speak the words "Our Father," heaven pays attention because we are His children. And as children, heirs of God through Christ (see Gal. 4:4-7), our privileges are enhanced by our Father's power. When we find ourselves in weakness or in need, a heartfelt cry of "Father!" gives us instant access to God and can send the angels scurrying, for they have been given orders to keep us in all our ways (see Ps. 91:11). The prayer of Jesus in the garden is a beautiful example. In distress of soul and perhaps with a wail, His voice uttered, "Father," and an angel appeared to strengthen him (see Luke 22:42,43).

TOUCHED BY AN ANGEL

As a father pities his children, so the Lord is tender and sympathetic with us. He remembers the weakness of our flesh, but His loving-kindness and mercy are from everlasting to everlasting (see Ps. 103:13-17).

This truth became very real to me in the early summer of 1984. We had completed a large building program in early 1983 and had started another almost immediately. The scheduled July dedication date was bearing down on us.

I enjoy building, planning, designing and decorating, and I even get into some of the physical labor when we are involved in these projects. A building program, however, does not slow down all my other activities, nor does it lessen my other responsibilities; it just adds to them. I am a person of detail, note making and list keeping, and I am very exacting in my desire to get things right. Needless to say, during this building program I got very little sleep, had too many things to do and my brain went into overload.

For years my personal time of prayer and devotion has been very early in the morning. However, the hot summer days and the pressure of time brought the workers to the building site at 6:00 A.M. I kept up my devotional discipline, but day by day guilt was growing because I knew I was not really praying as I should. My mind wandered and my eyes drooped from the long hours, late nights and 5:00 A.M. alarms.

I will never forget one particular morning. Wearily I crawled out of bed, got my first cup of coffee and headed to my study. I slumped in my rocker under a cloud of self-condemnation. I had neither the strength nor inspiration to utter the first word of prayer. In desperation I reached for my Bible on the table by my chair and opened it.

The first words I saw were from Psalm 103:13,14:

As a father pities his children,
So the LORD pities those who fear Him.
For He knows our frame;
He remembers that we are dust.

Tears flowed as freely as a fountain. My mind joined my heart in exclaiming, "He understands. He pities me in my tired, miserable state. He knows I'm doing the best I can right now." The tears washed away my self-condemnation. Instinctively I leaned forward as thanksgiving and praise took its place. Just as I did, I felt across my shoulders a tender embrace from another world. Strength flowed into me.

I stood up a different woman. My smile had returned and my energy switch was on full throttle. No one—at least no one visible—was in the room with me, but I know what happened because I was there. My heavenly Father heard my heart cry and sent the touch of an angel to strengthen me.

This was not what we would call Kingdom praying; it wasn't power praying. It was a tired child's cry to a tender Father.

Since that time I have heard of several others who experienced a similar very definite, invisible touch. One woman related the story of walking to a podium too ill and weak to speak, then feeling a hand on her back that sent strength surging through her body.

In a prayer service led by Arless Glass in Grand Island, Nebraska, during the arduous trial of my sister's church school versus the state of Nebraska, Agnes stood alone on one side of the platform. Brother Glass asked all of us in attendance to lay our hands on the backs of those in front of us and pray for strength. A large and heavy hand pressed on Agnes's back. Surprised, she looked around to see if some minister had come to pray for her. She was still standing alone, the only person on that side of the platform. Her angel had come to strengthen her as she prayed.

FATHER TO THE FATHERLESS

The story of Hagar and Ishmael brims with God's tenderness and fatherly compassion. For the fatherless and those with no protector, the Angel of the Lord intervenes. Hagar is weeping, but it is the voice of her son that gets God's attention (see Gen. 21:15-18).

The first time my sister Agnes was visited by an angel so well defines God's tender care for His children. If you have read her book, *Angel at My Shoulder*, you are familiar with the series of stressful circumstances and tragic times she encountered.

Her initial visit with her angel was on a rainy night. Recently widowed, she had endeavored to gain some financial security with an investment into what seemed like a sound business venture. After a few weeks of mounting questions, she had attended a meeting on this particular night when the bombshell exploded, wiping out her investment. The "businessman" with whom she had invested her money turned out to be a con man. Other investors left the meeting as downhearted as she, but with supporting spouses at their sides. Agnes left alone and went home to an empty house. She later told me that she was crying so hard she could hardly see to drive. Pulling into her garage, she unlocked the door and walked into her den. Immediately she became aware of a presence in the house.

"I wasn't frightened, but rather comforted," she said. "In fact, without thinking I called out, 'Daddy, are you here?' I felt like my daddy had come to see about me. When there was no answer, I was so sure someone was there that I searched the house. Finding no one, I started preparing to go to bed. With a heavy heart and a worried mind, I soon flicked off the light and closed my eyes.

"As I lay there trying to go to sleep, I felt the weight of someone sitting down on my bed. At first I thought my little poodle, Amy, had jumped up onto the bed. As I moved to investigate, I realized that Amy was already asleep, curled up beside me. At this same moment of realization, I heard someone call my name. I answered. Then the message was spoken to my mind, 'I am here. You go to sleep.' Instantly I fell into a deep sleep.

"The next morning is when I put it all together. I knew—I really knew—that an angel of the Lord had visited me, and it was so comforting that it seemed as if my father were there."

When you pray, say "Our Father." All of heaven goes on alert at the cry of God's child.

CHAPTER FIVE

HALLOWED
BE THY
NAME

We have two very important reasons for honoring, blessing and glorifying the name of the Lord in our prayers. First of all, He is worthy to be praised (see Ps. 18:3) and worthy to receive glory and honor and power (see Rev. 4:11). Jesus instructed us on how to give that praise, glory, honor and power in the pattern prayer given to His disciples.

Another reason we should hallow the name of the Lord in prayer is because angels are guardians of God's glory. Where God's glory is, there are angels. When we exalt, honor, sanctify, praise and glorify the name of the Lord, angels are drawn to attention. And where angels are, God's commands are done (see Ps. 103:20).

The cherubim, an order of angel that we discussed in a previous chapter, seem particularly assigned to this responsibility of guarding God's glory. From the Scriptures we learn that one of their stationary positions is beside the throne of God, ever on guard (see Ps. 80:1). After the fall of man, cherubim were also stationed at the east of Eden to protect the access route to the tree of life (see Gen. 3:24).

Earthly symbols of cherubim have long been incorporated into the design of holy places. This was especially true concerning the Tabernacle and Solomon's Temple. Both the Tabernacle curtains and the inside veil between the Holy Place and the Most Holy Place were embellished with designs of cherubim (see Exod. 26:1,31). No one could enter the Tabernacle without passing between the symbolic guardians of God's glory. Inside the Most Holy Place, cherubim were placed in the protective position at each end of the mercy seat which was set over the Ark of the Covenant. It was from between these cherubim that God would meet and commune with man (see Exod. 25:18-22). The guardian cherubim were ever reminders of the awesomeness of God's glory. Before the blood could be sprinkled upon the mercy seat under the watchful gaze of these angelic guardians, the priest first had to offer incense with fire, a type of worship (see Lev. 16:13,14). Worship and the blood are prerequisites for approaching God's glory.

In Solomon's Temple where God chose to hallow His name, the doors and walls were adorned with carved cherubim. The ark was placed again under the watchful gaze and the wings of the cherubim in the Most Holy Place (see 1 Kings 6:29,32; 8:6,7).

From the pronouncement of the birth of Jesus until He ascended into heaven, angels attended Him. They even announced the birth of John, who was to prepare His way (see Luke 1:11-13). It was an angel who spoke to Joseph and told him that the child Mary carried was conceived of the Holy Spirit (see

Matt. 1:20). An angel spoke to him again to command him to go to Egypt to protect the life of the boy Jesus (see Matt. 2:13).

Jesus, the Son of God, was the brightness of God's glory:

And the Word became flesh and dwelt among us, and we beheld His glory, the glory as of the only begotten of the Father, full of grace and truth (John 1:14).

And as we have seen, where God's glory is there are angels.

In John 12, Jesus was troubled and cried out to His Father. Those standing near said the thundering response to this cry seemed as if angels spoke:

"Now My soul is troubled, and what shall I say? 'Father, save Me from this hour'? But for this purpose I came to this hour. Father, glorify Your name."

Then a voice came from heaven, saying, "I have both glorified it and will glorify it again."

Therefore the people who stood by and heard it said that it had thundered. Others said, "An angel has spoken to Him" (John 12:27-29).

On more than one occasion angels have been seen as they moved among a congregation. A most graphic illustration of our subject of discussion happened at Life Tabernacle in Houston, Texas. Ima Kilgore, my dear friend whom I mentioned earlier, told me of a woman's experience during one of their church services.

It was congregational prayer time and the people were standing. As it always seems, some were standing reverently but probably lost in their own thoughts. Others were praying rather half-heartedly.

Then, of course, there were those who were lost in praise and worship, oblivious to everything except the presence of the Lord. Angels were seen by a precious saint, moving in and around the people. Many of the people they simply passed by, but when they came to someone who was truly worshiping, they would stop and lift their hand over them as though to bless them. It is the nature of angels to worship. Their primary function is praising and blessing God, so it is understandable that the hosts of heaven, where God's name is exalted and hallowed continuously, respond to those who bless the Lord and revere His name on earth.

Three times in the Scriptures we are instructed to give the Lord the glory that is due His name (see 1 Chron. 16:29; Ps. 29:2; 96:8). Perhaps an understanding of this is what David had in mind when he wrote:

Let my prayer be set before You as incense,
The lifting up of my hands as the evening sacrifice.
Set a guard, O LORD, over my mouth;
Keep watch over the door of my lips (Ps. 141:2,3).

I know of no better summary for this chapter. When David prayed for God to set a guard over his mouth and to keep a watch over the door of his lips, could he have been reflecting on the guardians of God's glory?

CHAPTER SIX

THY KINGDOM COME

Of no other king or kingdom could it ever be said, "Of His kingdom there will be no end" (Luke 1:33). The angel Gabriel announced this phenomenal fact to Mary concerning her Son before He was born. This baby, to be called Jesus and born to a peasant woman, would someday be the King of an unending Kingdom. The angel of God declared it.

The biblical books of Daniel and Revelation give us prophetic pictures of the final days and the glorious fulfillment of this unending Kingdom. In his vision, Daniel saw the world empires come and go as participants in a pageant. Babylon, Persia, Greece, Rome—on and on they entered the stage of history and then exited, marching in time with Bible prophecy. Finally all thrones were cast down, dominions were taken away, and Daniel saw "One like the Son of Man" (Dan. 7:13):

> Then to Him was given dominion and glory
>   and a kingdom,
> That all peoples, nations, and languages
>   should serve Him.
> His dominion is an everlasting dominion,
> Which shall not pass away,
> And His kingdom the one
> Which shall not be destroyed (Dan. 7:14).

When Daniel inquired as to the meaning of the vision from an angel—"one of those who stood by" (v. 16)—the unending Kingdom was described to Daniel as "the kingdom forever, even forever and ever" (v. 18). A similar scene is depicted in the fifth chapter of Revelation.

In both these references, angels are present and involved. They are definitely "in the know" concerning God's kingdom. Their allegiance to the King is marked by a tenacious commitment to His kingdom. The failure of the heavenly coup reported in Isaiah 14 was only the first of multiple attempts to divert the ultimate purpose and rule of God. Lucifer desired to exalt himself above God's throne, and war was declared in heaven. When Lucifer and those loyal to him were cast out of heaven, the battle moved to the earth where it still rages today.

When Satan tempted Jesus in the wilderness, the angels were there. This, after all, was a bold attempt to obliterate the coming Kingdom. With all his temptations, Satan's underlying motive was to halt the advance of the Kingdom on earth. Jesus' resistance put Satan to flight, and the ever-present angels immediately ministered to Him (see Matt. 4:1-11). When the soldiers arrested Jesus in the garden and led Him to death on the cross, more than a dozen legions of angels—72,000 angels if, as it is generally believed, there were 6,000 in a legion—stood at attention, ready to respond (see Matt. 26:53).

The Bible is replete with accounts of angelic involvement in ushering in the everlasting Kingdom. Their work in this regard is vividly portrayed in the book of Revelation. Angels are always busily involved in Kingdom enterprise, but we see increased visible activity in this culminating account of the Scriptures.

As the absolute end of all things approaches and the everlasting Kingdom is coming into focus, it seems angels are everywhere, doing everything—making declarations, raining destruction upon the forces and allies of Satan, protecting the chosen, doing the mop-up work as the war winds down, and ever praising and worshiping God. More than 50 times we observe angelic activity in Revelation.

In Matthew, the angels are seen as gathering out of the Kingdom "all things that offend, and those who practice lawlessness" (Matt. 13:41), and the angels are portrayed as accompanying Jesus when He comes in His glory to set up His kingdom on earth (see Matt. 25:31). Angels are very involved in and committed to the kingdom of our Lord.

What has all this to do with the Lord's model prayer? Again, let me say we are to pray "Thy kingdom come" because Jesus instructed us to do so. When we pray for His kingdom to come, we are declaring whose side we are on, and angels mark those on the Lord's side in order to deliver them.

Much discussion has transpired concerning the mark of the beast, that final identification of those allied with Satan's world system. It is interesting to note that in Ezekiel 9:3-6 and Revelation 7:2,3 we see those who are marked by the angels for salvation. Similarly, in Exodus 12:23 the death angel, or "destroyer," recognized the mark of lamb's blood and passed over the Hebrew firstborn; those who were marked believed there was a way out of Egypt. Angels recognize the mark of the Lamb and intervene for those who believe God's kingdom will come:

> In Him you also trusted, after you heard the word of truth, the gospel of your salvation; in whom also, having believed, you were sealed with the Holy Spirit of promise (Eph. 1:13).

Three times in these depictions of the conclusions of the kingdoms of this world and the coming of God's kingdom, we note a wonderful angelic involvement with the prayers of the saints. According to Revelation 5:8 and 8:3,4, the prayers we have offered are present in the throne room of God. Our prayers are protected and used by the angels in the events leading to the establishment of the everlasting Kingdom. When fire from the golden altar is added to the golden censer full of the prayers of the saints, it is then poured out upon the earth with voices, thunder, lightning and an earthquake (see Rev. 8:5).

The prayers offered in Ezekiel 9:4 precede the emissary from God, clothed in linen, taking the coals from between the cherubim and casting them into the city.

When you pray, say "Thy kingdom come." The angels may use it as ammunition.

CHAPTER SEVEN

THY WILL BE DONE IN EARTH, AS IT IS IN HEAVEN

Prayer does not mean that we try to talk God into doing our will, but rather it is a way of getting our will aligned with God's will. When we truly pray according to His Word and His will, the angels become involved because they are committed to do His bidding. If the devil can interfere with the will of God, why can't angels intervene at His behest?

> Bless the Lord, you His angels,
> Who excel in strength, who do His word,
> Heeding the voice of His word.
> Bless the Lord, all you His hosts,
> You ministers of His, who do His pleasure.
> Bless the Lord, all His works,

In all places of His dominion.
Bless the Lord, O my soul! (Ps. 103:20-22).

When we pray the Word and the will of God, we have heavenly allies in His angels. The angels have authority and are described as mighty and powerful, but their power is limited to doing only the will of God. They are committed to His will. When we pray, "Not my will, but Your will," as Jesus did in the garden (see Mark 14:36), we are positioned to receive angelic aid.

We have already seen how the angel came to Jesus and strengthened Him as He prayed on that last night. According to Luke 22:41-43, the angel came as He prayed, "Not my will, but Yours, be done." The angel did not strengthen Jesus so that He could escape; He had already made it clear that thousands of angels were ready and alert to help Him. The angel strengthened Him so that He could accomplish the will of God.

I have always thrilled at the story of Deborah and Barak (see Judg. 4—5). How could Barak and the downcast, oppressed Israelites overthrow Sisera and his ironclad army? The secret is found out in Deborah's song of victory:

They fought from the heavens;
The stars [angels] from their courses
    fought against Sisera (Judg. 5:20).

The first "star wars"? The Hebrews' heavenly allies, God's angels, made the difference in the battle. The will of God had already been declared in this situation:

This is the day in which the Lord has delivered Sisera into your hand. Has not the Lord gone out before you? (Judg. 4:14).

The will of God was decided in the heavenlies and was accomplished on earth by corresponding activities in heaven and earth.

The Bible gives several accounts of parallel activity between earth and heaven designed to accomplish the will of God. When God declared sure victory for His children in battle against great odds, the word "discomfited," meaning to defeat in battle or to perplex, embarrass or disconcert, is often used (*KJV*) to describe what happened on earth as unearthly events transpired. Consider these reports of God's will accomplished in the earth:

> *And the LORD discomfited them before Israel, and slew them with a great slaughter at Gibeon* (Josh. 10:10, *KJV*, emphasis added). When the Israelites were under attack, an assault from heaven of great hailstones killed more of the enemy than were slain by the sword (see v. 11).

> *And the LORD discomfited Sisera, and all his chariots, and all his host, with the edge of the sword* (Judg. 4:15, *KJV*, emphasis added). In this battle, the earth trembled, the heavens let loose with a torrent of water, and the horses' hooves were broken (see 5:4,22, *KJV*) as the angels joined the battle to accomplish God's will on earth.

These events may be retold in Psalm 18, David's great song of divine deliverance:

> In my distress I called upon the Lord,
> And cried out to my God;
> He heard my voice from His temple. . . .
> Then the earth shook. . . .
> Smoke went up from His nostrils,

And devouring fire from His mouth. . . .
The Lord thundered from heaven,
And the Most High uttered His voice,
Hailstones and coals of fire.
He sent out His arrows. . . .
Lightnings in abundance,
And He vanquished [discomfited] them
(Ps. 18:6-8,13,14).

Verse 10 of this same psalm tells us that God did this as "He rode upon a cherub, and flew; He flew upon the wings of the wind."

I don't pretend to understand all of this imagery, but according to Revelation 11:19, in God's heavenly temple where the angels are in array by the thousands of thousands, times tens of thousands, there are lightnings, voices, thunder, earthquakes and great hail. Repeatedly in the Word angels are connected to phenomena of nature.

Psalm 78 recounts the plagues of Egypt and attributes them to angels of destruction, or angels who ministered woe:

He cast on them the fierceness of His anger, wrath, indignation, and trouble, by sending angels of destruction among them (Ps. 78:49).

Consider also:

You will be punished by the LORD of hosts with thunder and earthquake and great noise, with storm and tempest and the flame of devouring fire (Isa. 29:6).

There was a great earthquake; for an angel of the Lord descended from heaven (Matt. 28:2).

Fire and hail, snow and clouds;
Stormy wind, fulfilling His word (Ps. 148:8).

Compare the happenings in Psalm 18 when God in His heavenly temple heard David's cry, to the description of what was seen in God's temple in Revelation 11:19 and what happens in Revelation 8:2-6 when the prayers of the saints are put in the golden censer in the angel's hand and mixed with fire from the altar before the throne. In each of these instances, we get a glimpse of angelic involvement with our prayers to bring about the will of God in earth as in heaven. Lightning, voices, thunder, fire, smoke, darkness, hailstones—all of these are descriptive of fervent angelic action at God's commands to accomplish His will on earth.

Worship is the primary function of the host of heaven, so is it any wonder, when Jehosaphat and all of Judah made praise a priority as they faced their day of terror, that the Lord set ambushes (the Hebrew word means something or someone lying in wait) against their enemies (see 2 Chron. 20:21-22)? Could those who were lying in wait have been angels?

CHAPTER EIGHT

GIVE US THIS DAY OUR DAILY BREAD

The miraculous provision of food in circumstances of great need is an often-repeated occurrence in the Bible. And on several occasions angels were involved.

One of the earliest instances of miraculous provision is the sending of the quail and manna to the children of Israel in the wilderness on their journey to the Promised Land (see Exod. 16; Num. 11). Manna, which in Psalm 78:25 is called "angels' food," appeared miraculously on the ground after the dew was gone in the mornings. Some Bible scholars interpret the reference to angels' food to mean either that manna is the actual food on which angels subsist or that it was food supplied by the ministry of angels.

The quail came as another miracle of daily provision. God walked upon the wings of the wind (see Ps. 104:3), and with the wind came a multitude of quail, which are very small birds. Imagine how many quail it would take to feed the millions of Israelites! There were so many quail that they covered a day's journey beyond the camp.

How do we know the difference between the works of God and those deeds performed by angels? Is there a line of distinction between the two? Only God knows.

God's Word is creative and it is settled. God cannot lie; what He speaks always comes to pass. When He speaks, angels rush to obey His commands. So I doubt if our human minds could ever delineate the difference between God's performance and angelic activity.

I love the mental picture I get when thinking of the innumerable little wafers of manna and the multitude of small quail it took to give the millions of Israelites their "daily bread." Maybe God just spoke it into being and it came from nowhere, or maybe there were innumerable angels spreading the table with manna as another multitude of angels pushed the quail with a wind into the camp. Either way, in that desolate wilderness men ate angels' food.

The psalmist asked, "Can God prepare a table in the wilderness? . . . Can He give bread also? Can He provide meat for His people?" (Ps. 78:19,20). The answer is He did!

MEALS ON WINGS

Elsewhere in the Bible we see a number of miraculous deliveries of food coming from God that could well have been by angelic involvement. For example, the prophet Elijah was tired, distressed, depressed, running for his life. Exhausted, he lay down under a juniper tree and slept. Twice an angel awakened him to eat a miraculously supplied meal in the wilderness (see 1 Kings 19:5-8). Good food—great service!

When Jesus finished 40 days of fasting and prayer in the wilderness, which concluded with His recorded temptation by Satan, the angels came and ministered to Him (see Matt. 4:11). What does this mean? The Scripture gives no full explanation, but perhaps it included feeding Jesus. The angel fed Elijah when his strength was gone and he "went in the strength of that food forty days and forty nights" (1 Kings 19:8). Jesus had not eaten for 40 days and was hungry (see Matt. 4:2). I am sure the heavenly catering service was quite eager to minister to Him.

The deliverance of and provision for the children of Israel on their journey to the Promised Land took a continual series of miracles. The Angel of the Lord carefully guarded this perilous time. Three times, Moses was directly assured that the Angel would go before them. When Moses summarized this journey after arriving at Kadesh, he simply said, "When we cried out to the Lord, He heard our voice and sent the Angel and brought us up out of Egypt" (Num. 20:16). In Acts 7:35,38 Stephen gave reference to the Angel's involvement in the wilderness travels of Israel.

It is important to note that angelic delivery of "daily bread" is usually reserved for extraordinary circumstances. Angelic catering does not arrive at your doorstep every day, but it is comforting to know that, if necessary, God's angelic "hosts" are on the job.

THE LORD WILL PROVIDE

God and His angels know the way we walk, and they are committed to do whatever is needed for us to make it, whether our need is for bread or for blessing. After giving thought and study to this subject, my spirit soared while considering His watchful care, His incredible attention to details and the constant surveillance of His angels over the children of Israel as they made their pilgrimage. Be assured the Lord is doing the same for us.

One night, when my husband, Tom, was away preaching and the children were already asleep, I felt the loneliness of the burden of work to which God had called us as I climbed the stairs to go to bed. When I turned out the light, my room was engulfed with a darkness of spirit so thick I was paralyzed with fear! I cried out to God, and at that moment a glowing light entered my bedroom door. It glided across the floor to the foot of my bed then came up to rest beside my head. I instantly fell into a deep, peaceful sleep of contented rest. As I thought back on that incident, I was reminded of Psalm 104:2, which says that the Lord clothes Himself with light. And when the angel came to Peter in prison, a light shone (see Acts 12:7).

In 1953, as newlyweds serving in our first pastorate, we made the long drive to St. Louis, Missouri, to attend our denomination's general conference. Our money supply, at best, could be described as meager. We spent the week in a second- (more likely, third-) rate motel, eating at cheap cafés but happy just to be there. Then departure day arrived. After eating breakfast and paying the hotel bill, we determined that we had just enough money for gas, two hamburgers and two Cokes for the 600-mile trip home. Being young, we gave no thought as to what we would do for money once we were home.

The day after we arrived, it became clear to me that a few things from the store would be necessary for us to make it through the weekend until the church received its next collections. My wallet was empty, so I checked all my purses, thinking I might find a little money in one of them. Nothing. I went to my husband and expressed my concern, but he could only confirm that he did not have any money, either.

Being a very thorough person, I went back to our closet and pulled down all of my purses. Once again, I began going through them. As I opened one of them, there in plain view was a ten-dollar bill. It wasn't much, but it was enough to meet the immediate need. No, it was not manna, nor was it quail, but bread and milk never tasted so good. I do not know whether this found money was a creative miracle, if my eyes were opened to see what I had previously missed or if perhaps an angel went before me into the bedroom to provide for us and then whispered to me to look again.

The following event happened during my teen years. My parents had left a thriving little church to pursue their burden to start a church in a new part of a larger city near where we lived. Dad, a carpenter by trade, was going back to work while establishing this new congregation. One Saturday afternoon as I walked down the hall, which in our home was adjacent to the kitchen, I overheard my mother say to my father, "E. W., I don't have anything to fix for dinner tomorrow. Do you have any money?"

"No, I don't," my father answered. "We will just have to pray about it."

Soon we all left in the car to do some visitation prior to the Sunday services. We returned home to find on our front porch several brown-paper grocery bags full of all the "fixings" for a wonderful, traditional southern Sunday dinner—roast beef, peas, carrots, rolls—all left by a man known as the neighborhood drunk. Why did he do it? I don't know and he never told. But I do know that the Angel of the Lord gave a command to a donkey once (see Num. 22:22-35), so I can certainly believe that an angel can direct a drunk.

One of my favorite personal stories again involves my oldest sister, Agnes. When she was a little girl, somewhere around the year 1925, my mother and dad were preaching throughout Texas. Times were tough and folks ate what they had, not necessarily what they wanted.

Agnes, who had a child's appetite, came into the kitchen and asked Mother for a sandwich with bread and jelly. Mother explained that she had neither. Agnes left the house, but a little while later she came back to inform Mother that she had gone out, climbed up in their old car and prayed for bread and jelly. An hour or so passed. Mother was busily working in the house as Agnes played nearby. Looking up from her chores, Mother saw a little girl coming down the lane with a sack in her arms and asked aloud, "I wonder who that is and what she has?"

Without hesitation Agnes exclaimed, "That's my bread and jelly!"

And it was. The little girl said, "While my mother was praying, God told her to send you this jar of jelly and a loaf of bread."

Whether it is angels' food for the children of Israel or the prophet Elijah, bread and milk for newlyweds or bread and jelly for a little girl, I don't know where to draw the line to say that God simply provided or that He commanded His angels to take care of it. I do know that angels have been involved in such situations before and, if needed, can do it again. Jesus said to pray for our daily bread. If He said it and I do it, daily bread will come.

Chapter Nine

FORGIVE US

What do angels have to do with forgiveness?

In a rather strange reading in Exodus 23, Moses received the assurance that the Angel of the Lord was going to go with the Israelites out of Egypt as He led them out of bondage:

> Behold, I send an Angel before you to keep you in the way and to bring you into the place which I have prepared. Beware of Him and obey His voice; do not provoke Him, for He will not pardon your transgressions; for My name is in Him (Exod. 23:20,21).

In researching this strange statement of not pardoning transgressions, I have found explanations of its meaning to vary considerably and become very involved theologically. However, for our consideration of how angels are involved with our prayers, it is sufficient to note that angels are aware of the transgressions of those they are designated to guide, instruct and help in their journey to the place prepared for them by God.

There is apparently no provision for the redemption of angels or forgiveness for any sins they may commit. At least we have no knowledge of a substitute sacrifice made to cover angelic sins. Accordingly, with their vast intelligence and knowledge, angels must be very sensitive to the need and possibility of forgiveness.

Jesus gave us some insight into how the angels respond to redemption and forgiveness:

> There is joy in the presence of the angels of God over one sinner who repents (Luke 15:10).

The arena of mankind, particularly the Church, has been referred to by scholar Kenneth Wuest as "God's University of Angels." Peter said that the angels desire to look into the mystery of salvation (see 1 Pet. 1:12), while Paul declared that one of the purposes of his ministry was that principalities and powers in heavenly places might understand by the Church the manifold wisdom of God (see Eph. 3:10). The angels shouted for joy at creation, and now all heaven and its angels rejoice exuberantly at the greater miracle of created, fallen man praying for forgiveness and being translated from the kingdom of darkness into the kingdom of light. Forgiveness is a magnetic mystery to angels; they are fascinated and observe it closely.

When Daniel entered into the intense prayer of repentance for the transgressions of his people an angel came to him:

"O Lord, hear! O Lord, forgive! . . . " Now while I was speaking, praying, and confessing my sin and the sin of my people . . . while I was speaking in prayer, the man Gabriel . . . being caused to fly swiftly, reached me. . . . and talked with me (Dan. 9:19-22).

After Moses, who had been falsely blamed and accused by the people, prayed to God for forgiveness for the children of Israel, he again received the assurance that the Angel would attend him (see Exod. 32:30-34).

When Jacob made preparation to return home and right the relationship with his brother, Esau, the angels of God met him (see Gen. 32:1). This encounter resulted in the specific blessing Jacob received when the Angel pronounced him a prince who had power with God and man (see Gen. 32:28, *KJV*).

CHAPTER TEN

LEAD US NOT INTO TEMPTATION, BUT DELIVER US FROM EVIL

When we pray this phrase of the Lord's pattern prayer, we are not pleading with God not to lead us into temptation Himself, for "God cannot be tempted by evil, nor does He Himself tempt anyone" (Jas. 1:13). Rather, it is a request that He lead us in a direction away from temptation and keep us from the evil one. How are angels involved in this aspect of our prayers?

Consider two of the most well-known Scriptures pertaining to angels and their concern and care for us:

> Because you have made the LORD, who is my refuge,
> Even the Most High, your dwelling place,
> No evil shall befall you,
> Nor shall any plague come near your dwelling;
> For He shall give His angels charge over you,
> To keep you in all your ways.
> He shall call upon Me, and I will answer him;
> I will be with him in trouble;
> I will deliver him (Ps. 91:9-11,15).

> The angel of the Lord encamps all around those who fear Him, and delivers them (Ps. 34:7).

Incidents of angelic leading, guidance, deliverance and protection are numerous in the Scriptures. Several times in this book we have considered how the angels were encamped around the children of Israel during the perils of their wanderings. Isaiah summed it up very well: "The Angel of His Presence saved them" (Isa. 63:9).

All the way back to the angelic visit with Abraham in the plains of Mamre and his prayers of intercession for Sodom and Gomorrah (see Gen. 18,19), the angelic deliverance of Lot and his family from the destruction of Sodom (see Gen. 19), the angelic intervention at the offering of Isaac (see Gen. 22), the angelic guidance in selecting a wife for Isaac (see Gen. 24) and the care and keeping of Jacob (see Gen. 32), the evidence of the Word is there: Angels are busily involved in our lives, leading us and keeping us from evil.

In faraway, heathen Babylon where there was no house of worship, no teaching priest and no godly family, the angels did not lose track of their charges—Daniel, Shadrach, Meshach and Abed-Nego. All testified that God sent His angel and delivered them from the evil forces that sought to destroy them (see Dan. 3:28; 6:22).

The evil one, it seems, often works through a personality of power who seeks to destroy the righteous. Herod the Great was such a man. In order to preserve his earthly kingdom, he sought to destroy the child Jesus. The Magi were warned of Herod's evil intentions in a dream, and an angel gave Joseph instructions to go to Egypt for the protection of young Jesus. Joseph and his family remained in Egypt until word came again from an angel to return (see Matt. 2:12,13).

Years later, neither powers nor jails with chains and iron doors could deter God's angel from delivering the apostle Peter from the evil proposed for him. Herod, the grandson of Herod the Great, arrested Peter, intending to kill him as he had his fellow apostle James:

> Peter was therefore kept in prison, but constant prayer was offered to God for him by the church. . . . That night Peter was sleeping, bound with two chains between two soldiers. . . .
>
> Now behold, an angel of the Lord stood by him, and a light shone in the prison; and he struck Peter on the side and raised him up, saying, "Arise quickly!" And his chains fell off his hands (Acts 12:5-7).

In the middle of a fierce storm, without one star to steer by, Paul's ship was lost and the evil one sought to destroy the apostle before he reached Rome. Neither the ship's captain nor the crew knew where they were. All hope was gone; destruction seemed imminent. Suddenly an angel appeared, took charge and delivered Paul (see Acts 27:13-26).

SPECIAL DELIVERY

I am reminded of a story about my late friend Dave Wright. In a Beechcraft Bonanza plane, he and his friend Eddy Wiese were returning home to Fort Worth, Texas, from Oklahoma, where they had attended a church service. They were reluctant to fly because of threatening weather, but with the assurance of the accompanying prayers of the saints there in Oklahoma, they took off into the sky.

The trip was uneventful until a thunderstorm started to gain momentum just as they were preparing to land. A strong downdraft caught the plane, dipping the left side into a power line and catching a wheel on the wire. There was a crash, followed by engulfing flames. With a minor cut the only injury between them, both men were able to run to safety. At a distance they looked back, expecting to see the plane explode. What they saw were two very large men dressed in grayish white robes and hovering over the plane, peering into the flames. Guardian angels, both survivors concluded—angels delivering them from destruction.

At times, God goes to extremes to lead us from temptation and deliver us from evil. Balaam insisted on pursuing what he wanted to do regardless of God's word to him. The Angel of the Lord became his adversary and obstacle in an attempt to try to stop his pursuit of evil. Blinded by his own will, he blamed a stubborn mule for hindering and hurting him, while all the time it was the Angel of the Lord trying to lead and deliver him from evil (see Num. 22:22-35). In these modern times we may not contend with a mule, but when we sincerely pray for direction, hindrances as well as opportunities may be God's will and angelic intervention for us.

Sennacherib's siege of Judah under Hezekiah's reign was terrifying and paralyzing, but divine intervention brought victory:

And it came to pass on a certain night that the angel of
the LORD went out, and killed in the camp of the
Assyrians one hundred and eighty-five thousand; and
when people arose early in the morning, there were the
corpses—all dead (2 Kings 19:35).

One warring angel alone killed 185,000 enemy troops to deliver God's people from the hands of this fearsome enemy.
Amazingly, Hezekiah's prayer (recorded in 2 Kings 19:15-19 and
again in Isaiah 37:16-20), which brought God's mighty deliverance, loosely follows the same pattern as the Lord's prayer. Can we
ever doubt that angels are involved in leading and delivering us?

As the old saying goes, "God moves in mysterious ways, His
wonders to perform." In reflecting on the miraculous march of
Israel from Egypt to Canaan, we marvel at the leading of the pillar of cloud by day and the pillar of fire by night.

And the LORD went before them by day in a pillar of
cloud to lead the way, and by night in a pillar of fire to
give them light, so as to go by day and night (Exod.
13:21).

And the Angel of God, who went before the camp of
Israel, moved and went behind them; and the pillar of
cloud went from before them and stood behind them.
So it came between the camp of the Egyptians and the
camp of Israel (Exod. 14:19,20).

Was this mighty pillar simply a cloud? An angel? A manifestation of God Himself? I do not know for certain. I do know it
was a supernatural act of God. And I also know that, according
to the Bible, the cloud guided, directed and protected the

children of Israel and that it is here referred to as "the Angel." What a wonderful example of angelic work: a supernatural act of God to lead His people, not into temptation, but to deliver them from evil.

CHAPTER ELEVEN

THINE IS THE KINGDOM, POWER AND GLORY FOREVER

The Lord's prayer, which was given to us for our instruction, peaks with a definitive ending, a declaration of utter triumph:

> For Yours is the kingdom and the power and the glory forever. Amen (Matt. 6:13).

We cannot doubt that angels rejoice at this declaration every time it is manifested or spoken. At the dawn of creation, when the foundations of the earth were laid, the angels sang together and shouted for joy at the display of God's might (see Job 38:7). At the giving of the Law on Mt. Sinai, 10,000 "saints" (believed by many theologians to be angels) witnessed the event with awe (see Deut. 33:2). At the birth of Jesus, the announcing angel was suddenly joined by "a multitude of the heavenly host praising God and saying, 'Glory to God in the highest, and on earth peace, goodwill toward men!'" (Luke 2:13,14).

It seems the angels like to be there in large numbers when God shows evidence of His kingdom, His power and His glory. When He created this world, when He gave it government, when He sent the Redeemer, the angels were exuberant. When God finishes the work of this world and hails the beginning of the unending glorious reign of the King of kings and Lord of lords, we see through the telescope of prophecy another awesome sight as the angels give lavish, extravagant praise and worship to the culminating coronation of time. The crescendo heightens from Revelation 4 through chapter 19. In the opening scene of the eternity that is to come, before the throne are angelic beings declaring:

You are worthy, O Lord, to receive glory and honor and power; for You created all things, and by Your will they exist and were created (Rev. 4:11).

Then I looked, and I heard the voice of many angels around the throne . . . saying with a loud voice: "Worthy is the Lamb who was slain to receive power and riches and wisdom, and strength and honor and glory and blessing!" (Rev. 5:11,12).

All the angels stood around the throne . . . saying: "Amen! Blessing and glory and wisdom, thanksgiving and honor and power and might, be to our God forever and ever" (Rev. 7:11,12).

And there were loud voices in heaven, saying, "The kingdoms of this world have become the kingdoms of our Lord and of His Christ, and He shall reign forever and ever!" (Rev. 11:15).

Now I saw heaven opened, and behold, a white horse. And He who sat on him was called Faithful and True. . . . And the armies in heaven, clothed in fine linen, white and clean, followed Him. . . . And He has on His robe and on His thigh a name written: KING OF KINGS AND LORD OF LORDS (Rev. 19:11,14,16).

When we pray, "For Yours is the kingdom and the power and the glory forever," we have tapped into the wavelengths of heaven, and the voices of the mighty guardians of God's glory mingle with the voices of praying people.

PART THREE

ANGELS
AND
DEMONS

CHAPTER TWELVE

THE
END
IS NEAR

"Satanism," "Satan worship," "demon possession," "demonic activity." These words have made their way from the Church and ecclesiastical circles into the secular media. No longer are they considered mythical or mystical. Awareness of the world of spirits is recognized and accepted with little doubt, although with little clarity. Considering this and knowing that Satan responds to attention and takes advantage of fear, I offer a few pertinent observations.

The Old Testament mentions Satan only 18 times, all within the context of five separate situations. Only after Jesus came as the light of the world were Satan's activities clearly exposed. The four Gospels make more than 120 references to Satan, devils and unclean or evil spirits. All of these appear in confrontational yet clearly victorious incidents in the ministry of Christ, all of which take place over the last three and a half years of His life.

In the book of Acts we see only five incidents involving a direct reference to Satan, devils or evil spirits; these took place over a period of approximately 60 years. Four of these incidents had victorious outcomes (see Acts 5:16; 8:7; 16:16-18; 19:11,12). The fifth was different in that those confronting the evil spirits were not Christians (see 19:13-16). Confronting demons is always a dangerous thing to do; never go into it without Jesus Christ.

Jesus came not only to redeem man but also to expose and confront the deeds of our enemy, Satan. Confrontations of the demonic were much more numerous in the Gospels due to this showdown of power. Jesus said, "All authority has been given to Me in heaven and on earth," as His final recorded declaration in the Gospels (Matt. 28:18).

The book of Acts records fewer demonic confrontations, not only because Jesus had already made a show openly of His victory over Satan (see Col. 2:15), but also because He had declared the victory and had watched as His followers practiced and exhibited the transference of power to them.

> Then the seventy returned with joy, saying, "Lord, even the demons are subject to us in Your name."
>
> And He said to them, "I saw Satan fall like lightning from heaven. Behold, I give you the authority to trample on serpents and scorpions, and over all the power of the enemy, and nothing shall by any means hurt you" (Luke 10:17-19).

Not only have we, as followers of Christ, been given the means to cast out demons, but we can also expect the Lord's angels to come to our aid in battle.

The issue of where all power in heaven and earth resides has been settled (see Matt. 28:18). The war is won. Jesus came to destroy the works of the devil (see 1 John 3:8). In the book of Acts and beyond, the occupational forces (the Church) needed only to maintain the victory already won. Thus the incidents of demonic confrontation diminished greatly after the victorious resurrection of Jesus.

Therefore, with the New Age rage and the acute awareness of demonic activity in our world today, let us keep our balance concerning spiritual activity and warfare. In the book of Revelation, a magnified insight into the culmination of all things, John makes more than 70 references to angelic activity as compared to only 13 direct references to Satan or the devil—another great reminder that those who are with us are more than those who are against us!

THE PART WHERE I GIVE AWAY THE ENDING

The closing books of the Old Testament and the final book of the New Testament are a whir of angelic activity. Apparently, as God winds down an era in time, angelic activity increases. One of the national news magazines declared 1993 to be the Year of the Angels (not the then California Angels—they lost 91 games and finished fifth). This proclamation was based on the rapid acceleration of interest in angels. This interest, as I mentioned at the beginning of this book, continues to grow.

As Christians we can shrug this off, saying that much of the popularity of angels stems from a false New Age understanding of angels and their function. Then again, could this backlash be part of the deceiver's plan to blind believers to the approaching end of this age?

We must not discount the disasters caused by natural phenomena, the building tensions surrounding Israel, the rising
power of the nations around the Tigris and Euphrates Rivers
where Satan, the Prince of Persia, first stood against God's purpose in this earth and is now doing so again. If all we knew about
Adam and Eve's expulsion from the Garden of Eden or the
destruction of Sodom and Gomorrah came from newspapers,
we probably would not recognize the vital part angels played in
these events. There is no doubt that the angels are involved in
helping to fulfill prophecy, which even now we see unfolding
almost daily.

As you think on the frightening nature of world events in
these troubled times, allow me to reintroduce the thrilling awareness of a biblical phrase we do not use or hear often enough: the
Lord of hosts. That is, God and all His mighty angels!

The Lord of hosts is His name (see Isa. 48:2; Jer. 50:34).
Writing in a time of national crisis, Jeremiah used this name 82
times. Isaiah, writing in time of Israel's need, used the name 62
times. Haggai, Zechariah and Malachi all used this name for
God repeatedly. In Revelation, John often referred to the hosts of
angels.

We hear a lot of talk about the "end times" and the coming
end of the age. Are you worried about how it will all wrap up?
Fear not! Read Isaiah's prophetic report and rejoice:

"Lift up a banner on the high mountain,
Raise your voice to them;
Wave your hand, that they may enter the gates
of the nobles.
I have commanded My sanctified ones;
I have also called My mighty ones for My anger—
Those who rejoice in My exaltation."

The noise of a multitude in the mountains,
Like that of many people!
A tumultuous noise of the kingdoms of nations
    gathered together!
The LORD of hosts musters
The army for battle (Isa. 13:2-4).

The psalmist declared, "The LORD of hosts is with us, the God of Jacob is our refuge" (Ps. 46:7,11). Thank God that verse is written in the present tense!

The many descriptive names of God were given by revelation in time of need. No less than 280 times does the powerfully descriptive name of God "the LORD of hosts" appear in the Scriptures. *Jehovah-Sabbaoth*, or the Lord of hosts, is one of the compound Hebrew names of Jehovah (Lord). Abraham gave us *Jehovah-Jireh*, the Lord will provide (see Gen. 22:13,14). Moses gave us *Jehovah-Rapha*, the Lord that heals (see Exod. 15:26). But amazingly, *Jehovah-Sabbaoth*, the Lord of hosts, was introduced by a praying woman named Hannah (see 1 Sam. 1:11).

Hannah, a desperate, praying, weeping, worshiping woman of faith and praise, was pressured by the pain of personal problems that she could not control. But Hannah prayed. She turned her trouble, grief and torment into profound intercession. Her prayer was beyond the ordinary; the priest Eli did not even recognize it as prayer and thought her drunk. Her desperate prayer led to revelation of all the divine and heavenly power available for her need when she called on the Lord of hosts. Her weeping intercession was miraculously answered, and she altered history with her prayer. What a testimony to the power of a woman's prayers! What a testimony to the power of the Lord of hosts!

What prompted Hannah to such heights of appeal, to call upon "the LORD of hosts"? There is no record of anyone ever having used this title before in prayer. *Sabbaoth* is from the Hebrew root word that means "army" and the verb that means "to wage war."

What could a shepherd boy with a slingshot and stone do against an armed giant? When David faced Goliath, there was more involved than a rock and sling. "I come to you in the name of the LORD of hosts," he declared (1 Sam. 17:45). This name was enough. When David took the stronghold of Zion it was because "the LORD God of hosts was with him" (2 Sam. 5:10).

Paul assures us that spiritual war and attack will come, but we have a parallel force of power through God to pull down the strongholds we cannot handle with earthly weapons (see 2 Cor. 10:4). The Lord of hosts is with us!

The Lord of hosts is with us when the nations rage (see Ps. 46:6,7) and when there is war in the earth (see Pss. 9—11). The King of glory is mighty in battle (see Ps. 24:8-10); He fights and defends His people (see Isa. 31:4,5).

Why did Hannah call on the Lord of hosts? Faith's initiative enabled her to reach beyond the restrictions of present circumstances. Few had ever prayed as she prayed, but her need and her desire enabled her to reach beyond the ordinary. She boldly reached for the power of God in prayer. That power is still available to us today.

Abraham asked, "Is anything too hard for the LORD?" (Gen. 18:14).

Jeremiah answered, "There is nothing too hard for You" (Jer. 32:17).

Possibility in the midst of the impossible has been proven over and over again by people just like us. Usually it is because we are moved by desperate need to appeal through prayer according to our faith in the power of a God who is able to do more than we can think or ask (see Eph. 3:20). He can send His angels to deliver a message we need to hear, to minister to us, to protect us or to war on our behalf.

So look up! There is more available than what we can see!

"Be strong . . . for I am with you," says the Lord of hosts (Hag. 2:4).

If the Lord of hosts is with us, the majority wins!

OTHER
BOOKS BY
THETUS TENNEY

". . . FIRST OF ALL . . ." PRAYER

An excellent resource manual from the author and her daughter, Teri Spears. Here are creative ways to enrich your personal and corporate prayer life, lead prayer meetings, pray for your family and your world, set up prayer rooms, study and teach the Scriptures and influence your community. Comes in a user-friendly loose-leaf notebook format. *$22*

FOCUSED LIGHT, VOL. I

A concise but very powerful Bible study on prayer, praise, faith and spiritual warfare. This is an excellent resource for personal spiritual growth or for use with small or large groups. *$9*

FOCUSED LIGHT, VOL. II

Follow-up study on prayer, praise, faith and spiritual warfare. *$9*

BOOKLETS BY THETUS TENNEY AND TERI SPEARS

SEASONS OF LIFE

Thetus Tenney's most requested message! *$2.50*

FASTING

Simple and practical instruction concerning fasting. *$2.50*

TEACH ME TO PRAY

Simple and practical instructions for teaching children to pray. *$2.50*

THE BATTLE IS HOT, BUT
THE HONEY IS SWEET

Fight hard, but don't forget to stop for a little sweetness! *$2.50*

All prices include postage and handling. To order
materials or to contact the author, call or write:

Focused Light
P.O. Box 55
Tioga, LA 71477
Phone: (318) 640-9657
Fax: (318) 640-1843